TOKYO
DAY BY DAY

TOKYO

DAY BY DAY

365 THINGS TO SEE AND DO!

Happy New Year!

Lines for prayer like you've never seen

Harajuku

🚶 Meiji Shrine

Every year, over three million people pass through the Meiji Shrine in the first three days of January. The shrine boasts the largest number of visitors in all of Japan, but even so, it's worth braving the crowd to come on the first day of the year. It's extra cramped at this time, so it's best to get there at around 4:00-5:00 am. After prayers and offerings, head to Tonkatsu Mai-Sen, which is open on New Year's Day, for fried pork so tender you can cut through it with chopsticks. Start your new year with a full and happy belly.

📍 1-1, Yoyogikamizonocho, Shibuya-ku

🚉 Harajuku Station

📞 03-3379-5511

🕐 Sunrise to sunset

🚫 –

- Pick up the special *omikuji* (fortunes on paper strips), *Omigokoro*, which are written in the form of a poem.
- Give the Otomekusu tree, a symbol of safety within the family, a bow before you leave.

Buffet-style osechi is delicious!

Note: Buffet image for illustrative purposes only. Prices, duration of operation and food prepared are subject to change.

Go to a buffet for this year's osechi

Shin-Ochanomizu

✗ Hotel Ryumeikan Ochanomizu

Osechi are traditional dishes eaten at the new year, consisting of specific ingredients that each hold special celebratory meanings. So make a reservation for the extra-lavish *Osechi* Buffet (reservation only). Established in 1899 but refurbished in 2014, Hotel Ryumeikan retains a traditionally Japanese atmosphere. Here, indulge in top-of-the-line *osechi* prepared by professional chefs. Take as much of the massive shrimp or salmon roe as you could possibly want. *Mochi*-pounding events are also held, so save a little room for those.

📍 3-4, Kandasurugadai, Chiyoda-ku

🚇 Shin-Ochanomizu Station

📞 03-3251-1135

🕐 Check website

🚫 –

- Classic *osechi* like *kazunoko* (herring roe), *kuromame* (black soybeans), and *datemaki* (omelet mixed with fish paste) are all available.
- The Tea *Osechi* sounds interesting, too.

Breathtakingly
beautiful

The sun rising before the torii *is positively divine*

Oarai

Oarai Isosaki Shrine

Isosaki Shrine is well-known for its *torii* gate, standing majestically on a single rock. The gate, withstanding the crashing waves, has turned this spot into a symbol of strength. On the first days of the year, you'll want to get up early to see the sunrise here. The sun, rising slowly just beyond the gates, looks celestial, and so photogenic. Afterward, don't forget to climb to the main shrine to offer your prayers.

- 6890, Isohamacho, Oaraimachi, Higashi-Ibaraki, Ibaraki
- Oarai Station and 100 yen loop-line bus
- 029-267-2637
- Gates open/gates close
  Apr. to Sept. 5:30 am – 6:00 pm
  Oct. to Mar. 6:00 am – 5:00 pm
- –

- The view of the Pacific from the *torii* gates in front of the main shrine is also spectacular.
- On your way home, stop by Aquaworld Ibaraki Oarai Aquarium.

Visit if it's your "unlucky year"

A shrine to drive away bad luck

Asagaya

🚶 Asagaya Shinmeigu Shrine

This place offers calm to those fretting over the new year, and it's also where you pray to ward off bad luck, specifically for those whose "unlucky year" is coming up. If this is your unlucky year, you'll want to pay them a visit. The shrine will ward off the evil and unlucky spirits around you. After your prayers, pick up a *Kami-Musubi*, a protection charm in the shape of a lace bracelet. With its traditional Japanese colors and classic style, it's cute enough to wear as a fashion statement.

📍 1-25-5, Asagayakita, Suginami-ku

🚉 Asagaya Station

📞 03-3330-4824

🕐 Changes depending on season

🚫 –

• The *Kami-Musubi* comes in many colors.
• Unlucky years for men are ages 25, 42, and 61. For women, 19, 33, 37, and 61.

A winter jog feels amazing!

A spectacular spot for gentle jogging

Hibiya

🚶 Kokyo-Gaien Park

The Kokyo-Runs in Kokyo-Gaien Park are popular for their flat, easy-to-tread paths. If you're new to running, this is the perfect spot to get started. Of course, being part of the Imperial Palace grounds, it is also a popular tourism site. Also known as a Special Historical Site, Edo Castle, Kokyo-Gaien park is practically the welcome mat to historic Tokyo. It looks spectacular covered in snow, and history lovers won't want to miss out on Sakuradamon, the gate to the former Edo Castle that was named an Important Cultural Property in 1961.

📍 1-1, Kokyo-Gaien, Chiyoda-ku

🚉 Hibiya Station

📞 03-3231-0095
(Kokyo-Gaien Management Office)

🕐 24 hours

🚫 –

- Make use of the Marunouchi Bike & Run facility.
- A great chance to work on your fitness before the year kicks off for real.

Famously classy crepes

Photo by: taoaya

Truffles and caviar: the fancy crepe with extravagant ingredients

Gaienmae

✗ Parla

The crepes here outrank all others. Make room in your itinerary, because these upscale crepes prepared with premium ingredients are worth making a detour for. Sugar Butter Truffle is ¥1,800, Caviar and Sour Cream is ¥2,200. These pastry masterpieces are worth the coin. The Shot & Crepe, served with alcohol, is highly recommended. And addictive!

📍 2-10-1, Jingumae, Shibuya-ku

🚆 Gaienmae Station

📞 050-5892-7169

🕐 12:00 pm – 10:00 pm

🚫 New Year's holidays, other irregular times

- Take a pic of the Paris-inspired exterior.
- Try their Royal Milk Tea (¥900).

Try all the different shapes!

A scrumptious galette lunch in a vine-covered house

Shinsen

✗ Galettoria

This three-story building covered in Japanese ivy looks like it comes straight from the south of France. Here, you can enjoy traditional French-style galettes: a round, flat pastry with a variety of fillings. The health conscious will be glad to know that Galettoria uses seasonal, organic vegetables and fruits. The shape of the galettes changes with each filling, so make sure you've got your camera ready to take a few snaps. It's cold outside and tempting to stay cooped up, so why not take your mood on a trip to France.

📍	1-26-1, Shoto, Shibuya-ku
🚈	Shinsen Station
📞	03-3467-7057
🕐	11:30 am – 9:00 pm
🚫	Tuesdays

- Elevate the meal and have some alcoholic cider with your galette.
- The dessert crepes are a must-have.

Lifestyle shopping with an in-house restaurant

Making changes to your room for the new year? Come to Jiyugaoka

Jiyugaoka

🎁 Today's Special Jiyugaoka

This lifestyle shop in Jiyugaoka has risen in popularity in recent years. It's a great place to find some new items to spice up your life in the new year. If you're looking to re-evaluate your lifestyle, definitely pick up a few things at Today's Special. The original shopping totes are a great place to start, along with select food products from around Japan, and houseplants for your home. There is a restaurant on the third floor, and after shopping, you can taste the dishes you'll want to imitate at home.

📍 2-17-8, Jiyugaoka, Meguro-ku

🚃 Jiyugaoka Station

📞 03-5729-7131

🕐 11:00 am – 9:00 pm

🚫 Irregular

- Kitchen appliances, stationery ... they have everything.
- There are many other interior decor shops around Jiyugaoka.

A picturesque backdrop for selfie lovers

Walk hand in hand at the Venice of Jiyugaoka

Jiyugaoka

🚶 La Vita

Jiyugaoka is a stylish town throughout, but one corner of it, often considered Japan's "Little Europe," stands out from the rest. This area looks a world apart from its surroundings with its Western-style brick buildings, colorful walls, and the gondolas adrift in the canals. Everything looks like it's from Venice, down to the details in the street lamps and the signs in the streets. As you visit the organic cafés and leather workshops, take your loved one by the hand and enjoy your leisurely excursion.

📍 2-8-3, Jiyugaoka, Meguro-ku

🚊 Jiyugaoka Station

📞 03-3723-1881

🕐 11:00 am – 8:00 pm

🚫 Irregular

• Don't forget a group photo with the townscape as your backdrop.
• You can get a haircut while admiring the gorgeous scenery.

Watch your breath puff in the cold in front of Mount Fuji

Photo by: Lake Yamanaka Film Commission

Worship the snow-capped Mount Fuji

Mount Fuji

📷 Lake Yamanaka Panorama Deck

People of Japan have revered Mount Fuji as "the home of their hearts" since ancient times. This natural wonder is at its most mystical in winter, when it is dusted with a coat of snow. In the early morning when a white crescent graces the sky, against the blue sky at noon, or at dusk with its glowing sunset—any time is the perfect time to see Mount Fuji. If you're lucky, you might be able to catch Diamond Fuji in mid-October or at the end of February. Dress warmly, it's time to go to Lake Yamanaka!

📍 Hirano, Yamanakakomura, Minamitsurugun, Yamanashi

🚃 Mount Fuji Station and bus

📞 0555-62-9977 (Yamanakakomura Town Hall Tourism Department)

🕐 24 hours

🚫 –

- In fall, the fields are full of Japanese pampas grass.
- At the end of January, the Mount Fuji Snow Festival takes place by Lake Yamanaka.

A day trip
with a view
to die for

Nikko from 4,500 feet above sea level

Nikko

📷 Akechidaira Ropeway

This is another beautiful spot accessible as a day trip from Tokyo. After a three-minute lift ride you'll be able to see the mountains of Nikko from the Akechidaira Observation Deck at an altitude of approximately 4,500 feet. The place is well-known as somewhere to enjoy fall foliage, but the snow-covered winter wonderland is just as marvelous. You can see everything from Mount Nantai to the Kegon Falls, which drains from Lake Chuzenji. It's the coldest time of year, so make sure to bundle up before you go.

📍 709-5, Hosoomachi, Nikko-shi, Tochigi

🚃 Nikko Station and bus

📞 0288-55-0331

🕐 9:00 am – 4:00 pm
Note: Subject to seasonal change

🚫 From Mar. 1 to Mar. 15 for maintenance

- Get the beautiful view of Nikko all to yourself.
- If you're lucky, you may see Kegon Falls frozen over.

Bamboo stick lanterns from Akita

Note: Contents of the festival are subject to change.

A festival of Japanese heritage

Suidobashi

🚶 Furusato Festival Tokyo

One of the biggest events of the new year, this unique festival brings together entertainment and local cuisine from all around Japan. On stage, Giant *Nebuta* (warrior figures) from Aomori and *Kanto* (bamboo stick lanterns) from Akita make an appearance. In this carnival-spirited space, the National Rice Bowl Championship and the "Be still, my taste buds!" Toppings Market, where you can try from side dishes from all around Japan to top off your bowl of rice, are jam-packed with people. It's a feast for all the senses.

📍 1-3-61, Koraku, Bunkyo-ku

🚉 Suidobashi Station

📞 03-5800-9999

🕐 Check website

🚫 –

- The Tokyo Koenji Awa Dance and the Okinawa Eisa Dance are loads of fun.
- Hosted annually in mid-January.

Photo by: The Edo Tokyo Museum

The interesting history of the transition from Edo to Tokyo

Ryogoku

🚶 Edo Tokyo Museum

This museum will not only remind you that Edo and Tokyo are the same place, but will show you how it has changed throughout the centuries. It introduces and explains in layman's terms the history of Edo after Ieyasu Tokugawa's arrival. The permanent exhibition is split into Edo and Tokyo zones, where the history and cultures of each are reproduced with life-size and scale models. The life-size replicas of Nihonbashi from Edo and Ginza Street from Meiji-period Tokyo will take you back in time. History buffs will spend hours here.

📍 1-4-1, Yokoami, Sumida-ku

🚃 Ryogoku Station

📞 03-3626-9974

🕐 9:30 am – 5:30 pm
(9:30 am – 7:30 pm on Saturdays)

🚫 Mondays, Tuesdays following national holidays, New Year's holidays

- The miniature models of Edo are so adorable.
- The museum was renovated in 2018.

See if you can spot a kabuki actor after the show

A fun introduction to kabuki

Higashi-Ginza

⚐ Kabuki-za

January is when Kotobuki Hatsuharu Okabuki performances are held, so enter the Kabuki-za and experience this unique Japanese artform. Audio guides and subtitle guides are available for newcomers to *kabuki*, a form of classical Japanese dance drama with elaborate costumes and makeup. We suggest the one-act seats for first-timers. *Kabuki* performances comprise many acts, and can last four to five hours. With these tickets, you can choose to watch only one act, perfect for those who are just stepping into the world of *kabuki*.

📍 4-12-15, Ginza, Chuo-ku

🚉 Higashi-Ginza Station

📞 03-3545-6800

🕐 Check website

🚫 –

- If you're going to go, make the most of it and rent a kimono for the occasion.
- The seats on the east and west on the first floor are perfect for two.

It's so majestic in person!

Photo by: National Diet Building

A grown-up's field trip

Kokkai-gijido-mae

🚶 The National Diet Building

Not *that* kind of diet. This is where the upper and lower house reps of the Japanese legislature meet, and it's free to visit. You don't even need a reservation as long as you apply for the one-hour tour when you get there. Even if you are unfamiliar with Japanese politics, these gorgeous chambers are worth the field trip. Afterward, visit the nearby National Diet Library. There, you can find rare manga and books that are out of print, so go check it out.

📍 1-7-1, Nagatacho, Chiyoda-ku

🚃 Kokkai-gijido-mae Station

📞 House of Representatives:
03-5521-7445
House of Councillors:
03-3581-5111
Weekends and Holidays:
03-3581-0069

🕐 Check website

🚫 –

- You can see both the House of Representatives and the House of Councillors.
- Learn more about the prime ministers of Japan from the free pamphlet.

So real, it's scary

Note: The images shown depict wax figures created and owned by Madame Tussauds.

Meet (immobile) world stars

Odaiba Kaihin-Koen

🚶 Madame Tussauds Tokyo

This is the Japanese branch of the London-created attraction found around the world. Here, take commemorative photographs with Bruce Willis, Lady Gaga, and Johnny Depp. These figures are so realistic, it's hard to tell they're made of wax, especially in photos. Hug them, pose with them, and briefly feel like a celebrity. How exciting! Admire Marilyn Monroe, still beautiful after all these years, and give Messi a high five. What kind of pics will you take?

📍 3rd Fl. 1-6-1, Daiba, Minato-ku

🚉 Odaiba Kaihin-Koen Station

📞 03-3599-5231

🕐 11:00 am – 8:00 pm
(last entry 7:00 pm)
Weekends and holidays:
10:00 am – 8:00 pm
(last entry 7:00 pm)

🚫 –

• Nighttime visits are available.
• Make a wax figure of your own hands at the workshop corner.

Gaze at the jewel-like park from the Ferris wheel

Keio-Yomiuri-Land

📷 Yomiuri Land

Yomiuri Land's annual illuminations, the Jewellumination, is the staple of winter dates in Tokyo. Have fun on the rides and attractions during the day, and wrap up the night with glittering, gem-like illuminations. If you hop on the Ferris wheel, you'll be rewarded with a clear view of the entire park, and we suggest you don't miss out. The cold makes it perfect to snuggle up to your special someone, while you admire the brilliant lights.

📍 4015-1, Yanokuchi, Inagi-shi

🚉 Keio-Yomiuri-Land Station

📞 044-966-1111

🕐 Check website

🚫 –

- Jewellumination is held annually between October and February.
- Check out the sparkling dancing fountain show.

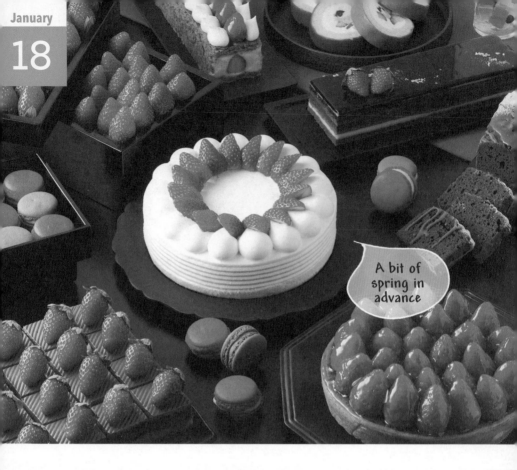

January

18

A bit of spring in advance

Strawberry picking, but in the genteel surrounds of a hotel buffet

Kaihin-Makuhari

✗ The New Otani Makuhari

Strawberry shortcake, strawberry tart, Napoleon, three types of strawberry parfaits of the day … wait, what? Is this strawberry-land? If you're someone who could eat strawberries all day, every day, pay a visit to this strawberry buffet. Savoury food such as sandwiches and roast beef are also available, so even those who don't eat strawberries will find something. This year, how about picking strawberries at a hotel? Prices start from ¥4,514 for adults (tax and service charge included).

📍 2-120-3, Hibino, Mihama-ku, Chiba-shi, Chiba

🚉 Kaihin-Makuhari Station

📞 043-297-7777 (representative)

🕐 The Lounge 10:00 am – 8:00 pm (Until 8:30 pm during dinner buffet times)

🚫 –

- Strawberry picking at the hotel is held between January and March.
- The mountains of strawberries alone are photo worthy.

Try a strawberry sandwich for something seasonal

If you love sandwiches, this is the place to go

Kami-Igusa

✕ Karina

Amidst the unprecedented sandwich boom of Japan, you can pick up a simple taste of nostalgia here. Karina opens at 6:00 am; it's so popular there's always a queue, and their signature egg sandwiches are often sold out by noon. The strawberry sandwiches, available only from February through March, are exquisite. Freshly made bread is lovingly sliced every morning, and generously stuffed with fillings. With sandwiches like these, the ¥200 price tag is hard to believe.

📍 5-19-6, Igusa, Suginami-ku

🚉 Kami-Igusa Station

📞 03-3301-3488

🕐 6:00 am – 2:00 pm

🚫 Mondays and Tuesdays

- The eggs are flavored with just salt and mayonnaise.
- Delectable sandwiches made with love.

January

20

Fall in love with live sumo wrestling

© Japan Sumo Association

The sumo wrestler merchandise is adorable!

Ryogoku

Kokugikan

The first sumo wrestling matches of January are called *hatsubasho*. The dull sound of large bodies crashing into one another will give you goose bumps when you see it in person. The live matches are incredible. The aptly named Sumo Dome and notebooks made in collaboration with major stationery makers are just some of the goodies prepared for your shopping pleasure. With this charming gap between the ferocious matches and the lovable merchandise, it's no wonder people grow to love sumo.

📍 1-3-28, Yokoami, Sumida-ku

🚃 Ryogoku Station

📞 03-3623-5111

🕐 Check website

🚫 –

- Aside from the matches, there are also events like photo sessions with the wrestlers.
- Drop by a *Chankonabe* (one-pot stew commonly eaten by sumo wrestlers to gain weight) restaurant in Ryogoku on your way back.

Relax in this homey atmosphere

An ideal restaurant for Kotatsu Hot Pot

Ryogoku

✗ Ryogoku Terrace

Hot pot at a heated *kotatsu* table: you might have seen it in manga or Japanese dramas. If you've ever wanted to try it yourself, you can at Ryogoku Terrace. The *kotatsu* seats are only available in winter, and you can choose between *sukiyaki*, *shabu-shabu*, chicken *paitan* broth, and other types of hot pot. Go with that special someone, and play footsies under the covers. Set the mood with one of the *chanchanko* vests (traditional Japanese garment) available for borrowing.

📍 1-12-21, Yokoami, Sumida-ku

🚌 Ryogoku Station

📞 03-5608-7580

🕐 11:30 am – 2:30 pm
5:30 pm – 10:00 pm
Weekends and holidays:
11:00 am – 10:00 pm

🚫 –

- Get in on the all-you-can-drink action for a comfortable drinking party.
- Try their summer barbecue terrace, too.

The hot pot you can't miss this winter!

Wrap the shabu-shabu *duck around the onions!*

Ebisu

✗ Torinago

Their signature dish is the Duck *Sukiyaki* made with fresh duck from Kyoto. Thin slices of duck are arranged like flower petals; it's so pretty, you'll want to admire it for a moment before eating. This delicious-looking duck goes for a dip in the duck broth *shabu-shabu*, before being wrapped around the thinly cut green onions. The broth is simple, yet packs a punch of flavor—you'll be amazed at how quickly it disappears. Suck up every last drop of that brewed-in umami by adding ramen noodles to the pot for the last course.

📍 1st Fl. 3-7-3, Ebisu, Shibuya-ku

🚃 Ebisu Station

📞 03-5420-1075

🕐 11:30 am – 2:30 pm
6:00 pm – 12:00 am
Sundays and holidays:
6:00 pm – 11:00 pm

🚫 Irregular; lunch times on weekends and holidays

- The *shabu-shabu* times are 15 seconds for duck, five seconds for onion.
- There is also a location at Sangenjaya.

The rice won't stop! The makgeolli won't stop!

Dipped in gooey cheese and sweet-spicy sauce, this is heaven

Shin-Okubo

✗ Sijang Dakalbi

Shin-Okubo is Tokyo's Korea Town. And, when it comes to Korean cuisine, nothing beats Cheese Dakalbi (dinner ¥2,678 for two persons). Chopped chicken and vegetables like cabbage and sweet potato are heartily stir-fried in a sweet and spicy sauce. On top of that is a generous serving of cheese. You'll want plenty to drink to wash it down. At lunch, rice, salad, side dishes, and soup are all you can eat. Talk about bang for your buck!

📍 1st Fl. 1-16-16, Okubo, Shinjuku-ku

🚇 Shin-Okubo Station

📞 03-3202-2400

🕐 10:30 am – 12:00 am

🚫 –

- Add a load of *dukbokki* for toppings.
- The Octopus Dakalbi is delicious too.

January

24

Come in and get warm

Warm up in a café with a fireplace on a snowy day

Ebisu

✕ Mercer Cafe Danro

You don't often see a café with a fireplace in Japan. First things first: warm your frozen fingers by the fire. For lunch, choose between freshly baked Danishes or pasta soups, or choose the Grown-Up's Kids Meal, made with premium ingredients. At night, enjoy iron griddle-grilled cuisine. The monochromatic, sophisticated space is perfect for a muted celebration. As you gaze at the gently flickering flames, you'll start to feel very sleepy. This café is full of comfort.

📍 2nd Fl. 1-16-12, Ebisuminami, Shibuya-ku

🚇 Ebisu Station

📞 03-3791-3551

🕐 11:30 am – 3:30 pm
5:30 pm – 12:00 am
Fridays, Saturdays,
days before holidays:
11:30 am – 2:00 am

🚫 –

- The fire is lit year-round.
- In winter, order a hot milk-based cocktail.

A café for tree lovers!

Have lunch under an enormous tree at this tree-café

Hiroo

✗ Les Grand Arbres

Les Grand Arbres is French for "The Large Trees." This natural and rustic mysterious tree fort of a café is famous for its appearances in TV dramas. The first and second floors are flower shops, and the third is the café floor. Here, you can order the Stay Pretty Menu or Unchanging Menu, both produced by culinary expert Ayako Sekiguchi. On sunny days, climb up to the rooftop terrace seats for lunch. You'll wish you had a café like this close to home.

📍 3rd FL. 5-15-11, Minami-Azabu, Minato-ku

🚃 Hiroo Station

📞 03-5791-1212

🕐 11:00 am – 10:00 pm
Sundays: 11:00 am – 7:00 pm

🚫 Irregular

• The Healthy Deli Plate is a must-have.
• The veggie-filled focaccia is also delicious.

A beautiful world of blue!

Note: Displays are subject to change

Enjoy a midwinter illumination show

Shiodome

📷 Caretta Shiodome

Shiodome is home to Nippon TV, and every year, the Caretta Illumination is held here. In 2017, the illuminations were based on the world of Disney's *Beauty and the Beast*. Not only are the visuals stunning, the choreography of lights and music sets an exciting, magical mood that is bound to move you. From the oyster bar on the second floor, Jackpot Shiodome, you can enjoy dinner while looking down at the illuminations. Book your seats early!

📍 1-8-2, Higashi-Shimbashi, Minato-ku

🚆 Shiodome Station

📞 03-6218-2100

🕐 Shops: 10:00 am – 8:00 pm
Restaurants: 11:00 am – 11:00 pm

🚫 –

- Illuminations start mid-November and end mid-February every year.
- Try the special menus at the restaurants in the mall.

Illuminations
for the whole
family

The winter illumination to see with kids

Suidobashi

📷 Tokyo Dome City

Here's another winter illumination. It's a part of the theme park at Tokyo Dome, so it's perfect for the kids. In 2017, the theme was "desserts," and illuminations like the Macaron Tunnel pictured above or The Dessert House of Light made appearances. During the event, you can purchase a special Evening Discount Passport that allows you to ride all the attractions for free. Have a blast Illumi-Riding on the colorful, light-covered Ferris wheel and roller coasters.

📍	1-3-61, Koraku, Bunkyo-ku
🚉	Suidobashi Station
📞	03-5800-9999
🕐	Depends on store
🚫	Depends on store

- Before the illuminations, take the whole family out shopping or to the movies.
- Held annually from mid-November to mid-February.

You've never been to a rink like this!

Skate hand-in-hand with your loved one

Roppongi

🚶 Mitsui Fudosan Ice Rink

Located in Tokyo Midtown, this seasonal ice rink lights up at night. Skate at night with your special someone, surrounded by glittering lights—how romantic! It's so clichéd, you might feel a little embarrassed, but just pretend you're in a movie and go for a skate hand-in-hand. Don't forget your gloves.

📍 9-7-1 and further, Akasaka, Minato-ku

🚆 Roppongi Station

📞 03-3475-3100

🕐 Check website

🚫 –

- They're also open during the day.
- Some hardcore skating fans go at lunchtime.

Perfect for beginners!

The ice rink with easy access for the whole family!

Kokuritsu-Kyogijo

🚶 Meiji Jingu Gaien Ice Rink

This ice rink is only a minute's walk from the station, and it's open all year round. The Olympic rink size (98.4 ft x 197 ft) means there's enough gliding room for beginners and experts alike. Head out with the whole family, get some exercise, stumble and laugh and work up an appetite. Then, on the way home, stop off and fill up with something yummy.

📍 11-1, Kasumigaokamachi, Shinjuku-ku

🚃 Kokuritsu-Kyogijo Station

📞 03-3403-3458

🕐 1:00 pm – 6:00 pm
Weekends and holidays:
10:00 am – 6:00 pm

🚫 –

• During spring break, lessons for beginners are available.
• Also open in summer.

Try a Totoro cream puff!

You'll want the Totoro cream puff so bad!

Setagaya-Daita

✗ Shiro-Hige's Cream Puff Factory

At a stand-alone shop in a residential area along the Odakyu line, you'll find four types of Totoro on display when you enter. At this shop, a mysterious pastry chef called Shiro-Hige, or White-Beard, makes these Totoro Cream Puffs with premium Japanese ingredients. We recommend the Totoro wearing the green leaf, Custard and Cream. Crispy puff pastry and mellow, rich custard galore!

📍 5-3-1, Daita, Setagaya-ku

🚆 Setagaya-Daita Station

📞 03-5787-6221

🕐 10:30 am – 7:00 pm

🚫 Tuesdays (open if holiday, closed next day.)

• Chestnut or strawberry-flavored cream are available depending on the season.
• Sit down for a while in the second-floor café before heading home.

Fun for the whole family!

The generous zoo with—gasp—no entry fee!

Hinodecho

🚶 # Nogeyama Zoo

The oldest zoo in Yokohama is, if you can believe it, free to enter. It might be small, but you can still come face-to-face with over one hundred species, big and small. There is a petting area, Nakayoshi Hiroba (literally "good pals plaza") that's perfect for children. The café in the zoo knows what parents want on their days off, and serve beer and wine with side dishes. Spend some quality time here with your family.

📍 63-10, Oimatsucho, Nishi-ku, Yokohama-shi, Kanagawa

🚃 Hinodecho Station

📞 045-231-1307

🕐 9:30 am – 4:30 pm

🚫 Mondays (open if holiday, closed next day); and from Dec. 29 to Jan. 1
Note: Open through all of May and Oct.

- Get your kid the popular Nogeyama Soft Serve.
- Don't miss out on animal feeding-time shows.

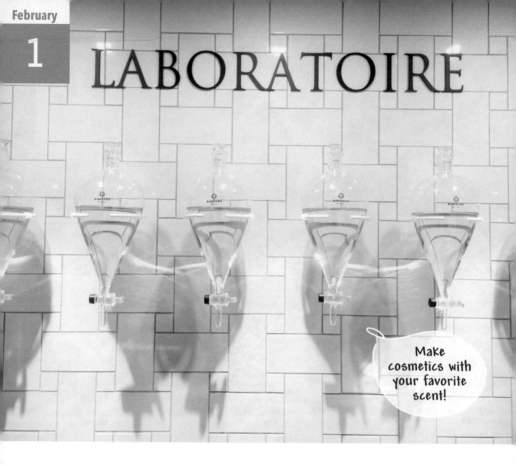

LABORATOIRE

Make cosmetics with your favorite scent!

The cosmetics shop where you can create your own scent

Omotesando

🎁 Huygens Tokyo

At this Paris-born cosmetics shop, you can mix your own organic cosmetics as well as choosing and blending your preferred scent. The store staff will assist as you pick from 15 types of scents to mix with body care or bath item bases. Make something for yourself, or craft something for your special someone. February 1 is Scent Day, so this is the perfect activity.

📍 3-9-19, Kita-Aoyama, Minato-ku

🚆 Omotesando Station

📞 03-6712-5522

🕐 11:00 am – 8:00 pm

🚫 –

• Make everything from body oil to shampoo.
• Everything is organic, and safe for your skin.

Mayonnaise lovers must visit!

Kewpie's fun facilities field trip

Sengawa

🚶 # Mayoterrace

The two red circles are actually a giant replica of an open Kewpie mayonnaise bottle cap at these facilities, which provide a fun and educational experience about Kewpie mayonnaise. Learn about their high-quality production process, the history of mayonnaise, the secret to Kewpie's tastiness, and grab a few tasters in between. When you get home, try your hand at recreating the mayonnaise recipes you've picked up. The visits are free, but reservations are necessary, so plan wisely.

📍 2-5-7, Sengawacho, Chofu

🚉 Sengawa Station

📞 03-5384-7770

🕐 Tours start from 10:00 am, 11:50 am, 1:40 pm, and 3:30 pm

🚫 Weekends, holidays and other temporary dates
Note: Saturdays are subject to temporary closure

• Pick up the limited mayonnaise bottles at the Kewpie gift shop.
• Participate in the mayo-making workshop.

Celebrate spring with a fat *maki* roll

If buying ehomaki *in Tokyo, buy it here*

Shimbashi

✗ Ginza Kyubey

Setsubun is the day before the spring equinox, when cleansing and evil-warding rituals are traditionally performed. *Ehomaki* is a sushi roll eaten for luck on this day, and this is the place to go if you want the most luxurious kind. Ginza Kyubey is number seven on La Liste, a list of the top 1,000 restaurants in the world. Their excellent *ehomaki* is generously rolled with conger eel, grilled egg with minced shrimp, prawn, shiitake mushrooms, and cucumbers. You'll be so busy eating you won't want to talk.

📍 8-7-6, Ginza, Chuo-ku

🚊 Shimbashi Station

📞 03-3571-6523

🕐 11:30 am – 2:00 pm
5:00 pm – 10:00 pm

🚫 Sundays, holidays, Obon holidays, New Year's holidays

- Take home some Bara-Chirashi, or assorted toppings on rice, to eat.
- Their *kaiseki* dinner course, Shigaraki, starts from approx. ¥16,200.

All kinds
of tofu

Fresh and delicious "treat yo'self" tofu

Nishiarai

🎁 Sugita Tofu

This traditional tofu specialty store was established in 1933.
The third-generation husband-and-wife team get to work at
four in the morning to make tofu treats full of real soy flavor.
The thin and thick fried tofu and tofu fritters are all so good that
customers keep on coming because "other places just won't
do." On a chilly winter day, how about some boiled tofu or
tofu *oden*?

📍 3-28-10, Sekibara, Adachi-ku

🚇 Nishiarai Station

📞 03-3887-2948

🕐 Early morning – 6:30 pm

🚫 Sundays

- Buy some tofu, fried tofu, and tofu fritter to make your own *oden*.
- Rich soy milk desserts are also available.

It's running off the grill!

Don't let the famous Japanese Black Hamideru Kalbi get away!

Gotanda

✗ Futago

Spot Futago by the red lanterns hanging outside. This chain is so popular it has thirty-four locations in Tokyo alone. Here, the dish you must order is the Japanese black *wagyu* Hamideru Kalbi (*hamideru* means to run off or stick out). This reservation-only, limited dish allows you to savor four slices of 8.8 oz. beef at once: the ribeye, rib cap plate, cuts from between the ribs, and kalbi. Every mouthful is a taste sensation. The overflowing juices are simply irresistible. Also, February 5 is Twin (*futago*) Day.

📍 1st Fl. 1-25-1, Nishi-Gotanda, Shinagawa-ku

🚃 Gotanda Station

📞 03-5434-2515

🕐 5:00 pm – 2:00 am
Weekends and holidays:
5:00 pm – 12:00 am

🚫 –

- Many guests come back for the fresh offal.
- Wrap up the meal with the homemade oxtail soup.

An innovative use of cotton candy

Meat on cotton candy! This is sukiyaki

Ginza

✗ Musashi-Bettei Ganryujima

Order the *sukiyaki*, and wow! A pot covered in cotton candy appears before you. Apparently the cotton candy is a replacement for granulated sugar. Turn up the heat and watch it melt like snow in a matter of moments: a truly amazing sight. So cute, even the most stoic of us can't help but crack a smile. Now, put your phone away and crack your eggs. Dig in!

📍 5th Fl. 7-2-20, Ginza, Chuo-ku

🚇 Ginza Station

📞 03-5568-5555

🕐 5:00 pm – 11:30 pm
Fridays and days before holidays:
5:00 pm – 5:00 am

🚫 New Year's holidays
(Dec. 31 – Jan. 3)

- Only A5-ranking Japanese black *wagyu* are served, and for a fair price.
- There are plenty of private rooms, so book for any occasion.

February

6

Sweetness is happiness

The Chocolate Factory Tour for choc-a-holics!

Nakameguro

🎁 Green Bean to Bar Chocolate

It's a week before Valentine's Day, and we're on the prowl for chocolate. Here, the chocolates are made in the traditional American "bean-to-bar" process. You can watch the entire process of cocoa beans transforming into chocolate from behind glass. Around this time of year, chocolate bars and candies, which take about forty-five days of careful crafting before hitting the shelves, come in seasonally limited flavors. Buy some for your partner, family, friends, or yourself. Perfect for gift-giving.

📍 2-16-11 Aobadai, Meguro-ku

🚉 Nakameguro Station

📞 03-5728-6420

🕚 11:00 am – 9:00 pm

🚫 Wednesdays

- Buy the chocolate bar (¥1,620 and up) for yourself.
- Try the bean-to-bar cakes and desserts, too.

Heaven for chocolate lovers

Satisfy your cravings with gourmet New York chocolates

Ginza

✗ Cacao Market by MarieBelle

Sweeten your day at the Cacao Market, a cozy café located in the luxurious and trendy shopping district of Ginza. Situated on the fifth floor of the Tokyu Plaza Ginza, the café's offerings include everything from their famous signature ganache squares, available in dozens of luscious flavors and intricate designs, to their rich "Triple Angel Gelato" topped with brownies. No matter what you're in a mood for, the Cacao Market is sure to satisfy!

📍 Tokyu Plaza Ginza 5F,
5-2-1 Ginza, Chuo-ku

🚌 Ginza Station

📞 03-6264-5122

🕐 11:00 am – 9:00 pm

🚫 –

- Limited-edition chocolates available for Valentine's Day.
- Hot chocolate is a must-try in the winter.

Handmade goodies are the best

To find new things for your new life

Gakugei-Daigaku

🎁 Claska

Bring a bit of Tokyo style back home—you might find just the right thing in this renovated hotel complex. Inside, you'll see a restaurant on the first floor, a shop and gallery on the second, and hotel rooms above that. The concept of the whole building is Living with Aesthetics, and you'll find new lifestyle ideas on every floor. Take home some handmade goodies you won't find in major retail stores.

📍 1-3-18 Chuocho, Meguro-ku

🚉 Gakugei-Daigaku Station

📞 03-3719-8121

🕐 Shop: 11:00 am – 7:00 pm
Restaurant: 7:30 am – 5:30 pm
8:00 pm – 11:30 pm

🚫 –

• Before you go, fill up on delicious French cuisine at the first-floor restaurant.
• Check for event and gallery show info before you go.

Photo by: Tono

Akihabara to Okachimachi, artisan space under an overpass

Suehirocho

2k540 Aki-oka Artisan

In Okachimachi, a town once known as a center for craftsmen, this posh facility for a new generation of artisans was born. What makes it special is that the workshops and storefronts are one and the same, and you can speak directly with the artisans at every store as you shop. From traditional Japanese crafts to bags and jewellery, even baby supplies, you're guaranteed to find something unique here just for you.

📍 Under the overpass, 5-9, Ueno, Taito-ku

🚃 Suehirocho Station

📞 03-6806-0254

🕐 11:00 am – 7:00 pm
   Note: Depends on store

🚫 Wednesdays
   Note: Depends on store

- Participate in one of the many workshops available, such as silk-dyeing.
- The wooden keyboards by Hacoa are super cool.

What's inside? Is it what you wanted?

Go on a capsule toy shopping spree

Suehirocho

🎁 Akihabara Gachapon Kaikan

This is the mecca of capsule toys, also known as *gachapon* or *gashapon*, where over five hundred machines line the walls and make up corridors so narrow, only one person can pass at a time. They have everything from the cute Cat or Fuchiko on the Cup series, to the more maniacal Orange Peel, Groveling Men, and Junji Inagawa's Haunted Photographs series. Yep, gacha all day, gacha all night. There's a surreal feeling about the place; these toys don't take themselves seriously, but will still touch your heart.

📍 3-15-5, Sotokanda, Chiyoda-ku

🚇 Suehirocho Station

📞 03-5209-6020

🕐 11:00 am – 8:00 pm
Fridays, Saturdays, days before holidays: 11:00 am – 10:00 pm
Sundays and holidays:
11:00 am – 7:00 pm

🚫 –

- Get those coins ready for a spending spree.
- Collect the "jackpot" stickers for free turns at the machines.

Holy cow, it really became lettuce!

Food replica fun for everyone!

Asakusa

Ganso Shokuhin Sample-ya Kappabashi Store

"Look, world!" At this specialty store, get some unique hands-on experience with Japanese craftsmanship. Here, you can make replicas of lettuce and your favorite tempura. Ease the colored wax into a sink of hot water and form its shape. It's more fun than you expect, and before you know it, your own food replica is complete. Seasonal workshops for realistic replicas of foods like waffles and ice cream are also available.

3-7-6, Nishi-Asakusa, Taito-ku (main store)

Asakusa Station

0120-17-1839

10:00 am – 5:30 pm

–

- Pick up magnets or keychains as souvenirs.
- You can buy the replica food in the windows.

2018 O

Get crafty, whatever your skill level

Valentine's Day gift wrapping at a "box store"

Futako-Tamagawa

🎁 Box & Needle Store

As you know by now, Tokyo is home to a plethora of specialty stores. This is the world's first specialty store for boxes, opened by a traditional paper container-maker from Kyoto. These boxes are lovingly hand pasted one by one, with paper selected from Italy, Finland, Nepal, and other places from around the world. You have square boxes, round boxes, boxes in every color and pattern and texture, and more. Give your Valentine their gift in your favorite box. This year, make something with your whole heart instead of giving something store-bought.

📍 3-12-11, Tamagawa, Setagaya-ku

🚉 Futako-Tamagawa Station

📞 03-6411-7886

🕘 11:00 am – 7:00 pm

🚫 Wednesdays

- You can also buy the paper with which the boxes are made.
- Join the jewelry box-making workshops.

A different way to make hot chocolate

Here, playing with your food is encouraged

Jujo

✗ Bonnel Cafe

Take a chocolate ball on a stick and dunk it in steaming hot milk. This melt-it-and-eat-it sensation, Hot Stick Chocolate (¥500), is just too much fun—it's like drinking directly from a chocolate fondue. It pairs perfectly with cookies or marshmallows, and is a fabulous way to warm up on a cold day. This is the café to visit with your friends for Valentine's Day.

📍 2-23-10, Kamijujo, Kita-ku

🚉 Jujo Station

📞 03-4296-7109

🕐 Lunch: 11:00 am – 2:30 pm
Café: 3:00 pm – 7:30 pm
Takeout: 11:00 am – 8:00 pm

🚫 Irregular

- There are four types: Milk, Milk for Grown-ups, Black Tea, and Cinnamon.
- Omelet rice and other savory lunch menu options are available.

Like opening a Japanese winter treasure chest

The Japan Nightscape Heritage Site at Kamakura Festival

Yunishikawa-onsen

Yunishikawa Hot Springs

Each year at this historic hot spring in Ibaraki, the Kamakura Festival is held from the end of January until early March. Along the riverbanks of Heike no Sato, over 800 mini-*kamakura*, or Japanese igloos, are built. At night, the candles inside are lit, and magical scenery softly appears in the darkness. A nice long look at this official Nightscape Heritage of Japan is a given, but we also suggest the reservations-only Kamakura Barbecue. Stuffing yourself with hot barbecued meat while sitting in a giant igloo is an extraordinary experience you won't find elsewhere.

- Yunishikawa Hot Spring Town, Nikko-shi, Tochigi
- Yunishikawa-onsen Station and bus
- 0288-22-1525 (Nikko Tourism Association)
- Check website
- –

- Try the thrilling snow rafting.
- Take a picture with the snowmen on the street.

Ice artwork so stunning you'll forget to feel cold

A beautiful icescape

Mitsumineguchi

📷 Misotsuchi Icicles

As spring approaches, an ephemeral work of art takes shape in Saitama. The icicles created by frozen spring water in the harsh temperatures of Okichichibu can only be described as majestic. During the Otaki Ice Festival, the icicles are illuminated with color, adding to the beauty. If you start to feel chilly, warm up with some hot sweet sake and the local specialty snack, Miso Potato, at a nearby restaurant.

📍 4011-1, 4066-1, Otaki, Chichibu-shi, Saitama

🚌 Mitsumineguchi Station and bus

📞 0494-55-0707 (Chichibu Tourism Association Otaki Branch)

🕐 Check website

🚫 —

- The Otaki Ice Festival is held between mid-January and mid-February.
- To visit, an environmental support fee of ¥200 is required for everyone over 13.

Take a few snaps and feel like a celebrity

The perfect pink backdrop for a photo

Suidobashi

🚶 Athénée Français

As you walk from the station, these pink walls jump out at you. Established in 1913, this is, in fact, the oldest French-language school in Japan, but it is also a popular photo spot due to its striking architecture. Sit down on the railings in front of the wall of alphabets and pretend you're a model. Even a low-effort shot will look super chic. Look for your initials, and take a picture with them, too.

📍 2-11, Kandasurugadai, Chiyoda-ku
🚃 Suidobashi Station
📞 03-3291-3391
🕐 9:30 am – 7:30 pm
🚫 Sundays and school holidays

- Act like you're at the Paul Smith wall in L.A.
- Watch a French film at the school while you're here.

Have some tequila in a pink world

Mexican cuisine with the cutest of skeletons

Shibuya

✗ Texmex Factory

If you think the entrance is photo worthy, wait until you step inside. A pink skeleton made of neon lights is waiting to greet you in this Mexican restaurant. The painted Pink Room is perfect for a girls' night out. In this moody, exciting space, make short work of popular dishes like tacos, burritos, and fajitas, and wash them down with some Corona or tequila-based cocktails.

📍 2nd Fl. 1-19-3, Jinnan, Shibuya-ku

🚇 Shibuya Station

📞 03-5459-3690

🕐 11:30 am – 12:00 am

🚫 Wednesdays

- The chairs and walls and all of the décor are so photogenic.
- The burritos are a must-have.

February
19

博物館
POLICE MUSEUM

POLICE HELICOPTER "OT
AgustaW
L:16.62r

POLICE VEHICLE
TOYOTA CROWN210
L:4.93m W:1.80m H:1.81m

Your heart might pound a bit even if you haven't broken any laws

---

Behind the scenes of Tokyo Police

Kyobashi

🚶 Police Museum

This is a hands-on museum run directly by the Metropolitan Police Department of Tokyo. The history of the Tokyo Police, from the Meiji period to the newest crime-fighting know-how, fills every corner of this seven-floor building. Even grown-ups will be excited by the opportunity to test-ride police motorcycles and helicopters, try dusting for fingerprints, and even experience an emergency call. The best part? It's free. Go on, enter—you haven't done anything wrong, right?

📍 3-5-1, Kyobashi, Chuo-ku

🚇 Kyobashi Station

📞 03-3581-4321 (Metropolitan Police Representative)

🕐 9:30 am – 5:00 pm

🚫 Mondays (open if holiday, closed next day), New Year's holidays

---

• Definitely ride the motorcycle and helicopter.
• If visiting with children, take them to try on the uniforms.

They can turn your photos into a globe!

Turn your precious memories into a treasure dome of glass

Ikejiri-Ohashi

Snowdome Museum

This is the only art museum in the world with a permanent exhibition of snow globes. The fluttering snow in the glass domes are a magical, tiny universe of comforting nostalgia. Over 1,500 snow globes collected from around the world are on display. Here, you can create your very own snow globe in their workshop (¥3,900 and up). By the way, February 20 is Snow Globe Appreciation Day.

📍 No. 109, 2-4-5, Ikejiri, Setagaya-ku

🚉 Ikejiri-Ohashi Station

📞 03-5433-0081

🕐 11:00 am – 5:00 pm

🚫 Mondays

- You can also order original snow globes.
- Imported snow globes from around the world are also available for purchase.

Ile-de-France
39 RUE DE PARIS
This is quite the view!

The poshest and most comfortable cat café

Akihabara

Cat Café Mocha

Missing your cat while you're away? If you're a cat lover who is longing for the touch of soft, fluffy fur and squishy paw pads, come to Mocha. The cats lounge comfortably in a living-room-style café with large, sunny windows. With single seats, double-seaters for friends or couples, and free Wi-Fi, you can spend your time leisurely here (¥216 per hour, all-you-can-drink service extra). Fill up your camera with endearing portraits of cats before you leave.

- 2nd Fl. 4-4-3, Sotokanda, Chiyoda-ku
- Akihabara Station
- 03-5577-5399
- 10:00 am – 10:00 pm (last entry 9:30 pm)
- –

- Be there for the two daily feeding times at 10:30 am and 7:30 pm.
- Work surrounded by cats (Wi-Fi, power ports available).

Too cute, fur real

Adorable 3-D cat latte art

Oshiage

✕ Oshiage Nyanko

This store is a café during the day and becomes a bar, Oshiage Bunko, in the evening. While there are no real cats, the whole café is a shrine to felines, present in the form of decorations and miscellaneous goodies. Most importantly, the 3-D Cat Art Drink is so precious, it'll make you crack a smile at first glance. The cat looks like it'll get up and move at any moment; you almost won't want to drink it. By the way, today is Cat Day.

📍 Inside Oshiage Bunko, 3-10-9, Oshiage, Sumida-ku

🚆 Oshiage Station

📞 03-3617-7471

🕐 12:00 pm – 5:00 pm (last order 4:30 pm)

🚫 Mondays to Wednesdays

- Find the store by its cat-patterned shop curtains.
- The *Matcha* Soy Au Lait looks like a cat resting on grass.

A stitcher's winter sounds fun, too

The place to go for textile lovers

Daikanyama

🎁 Cocca

These textiles may look Scandinavian, but this intriguing fabric shop is actually 100 percent Japanese-designed and produced. Bags or socks, umbrellas or drawstring pouches, the items born from the infinite possibilities of a piece of textile enrich your life in the subtlest of ways. How about picking up some fabric and starting a new hobby as a stitcher for the coming season? Also, you should know that February 23 is *Furoshiki* (Japanese wrapping cloth) Day.

📍 1-31-13, Ebisunishi, Shibuya-ku

🚉 Daikanyama Station

📞 03-3463-7681

🕐 11:00 am – 7:00 pm

🚫 Mondays

- There's always an exhibition to check out.
- While you're at it, buy some threads and needles to complete your sewing kit.

Winter is coming to a close

Visit the god of scholars and purify your heart with plum blossoms

Yushima

🚶 Yushima Tenjin Shrine

Enshrined here is Sugawara no Michizune, known as the god of scholars. It's so popular that during exam season, about fifty thousand *ema* are hung in prayer each year. But it is also famous for its plum blossoms. The plum flowers begin to bloom fully around mid-February, and the blossoms of around three hundred trees of twenty species of plum are yours to take in. During the Plum Blossom Festival, events like commodity fairs and live harp performances take place, so head out there and enjoy the interval between winter and spring.

📍 3-30-1, Yushima, Bunkyo-ku

🚃 Yushima Station

📞 03-3836-0753

🕐 Doors open: 6:00 am – 8:00 pm
Charm and prayer booth:
8:30 am – 7:30 pm

🚫 –

- The Plum Festival is held between February and March.
- Pet the *Nade-Ushi* (literally "petting bull") for good health.

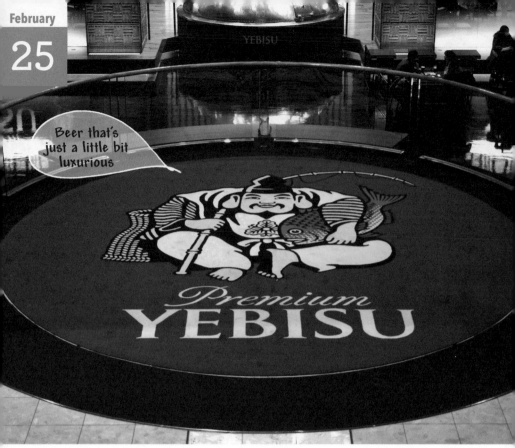

Beer that's just a little bit luxurious

Premium
YEBISU

Photo by: Sapporo Beer

On Ebisu day, obviously have Yebisu beer!

Ebisu

🚶 Museum of Yebisu Beer

This is a playground for adults in Ebisu Garden Place. On the Yebisu Beer Tour, learn all about the history of beer and pick up some trivia. After that, it's tasting time. Learn how to best enjoy beer while you try the two types available. In the tasting salon (for which there is a separate entry fee), you can enjoy two types of Yebisu beer on tap, and cocktails made with Yebisu beer.

📍 4-20-1, Ebisu, Shibuya-ku

🚃 Ebisu Station

📞 03-5423-7255

🕐 11:00 am – 7:00 pm (Last times for the Yebisu Tour: weekdays 5:10 pm, weekends and holidays 5:30 pm)

🚫 Mondays (open if holiday, closed next day), New Year's holidays, some other irregular days (call first)

- It's free if you just want to visit.
- Take home some of the rare, original Yebisu merchandise.

Whew!

The fun, free brewery (and tasting) tour for adults

Namamugi

🚶 Kirin Brewery Yokohama

Factory tours are all the rage right now and breweries are some of the most fun. Follow your guide through the production process, try the malt, and taste test the wort from different stages of production. Not only do you get to observe, but also experience beer brewing with all five senses. After the tour is done it's time for—you guessed it—the free draft beer tasting time you've been waiting for. Have fun getting a foam mustache! We also recommend the restaurant, where you can have both regular barbecue and Mongolian mutton barbecue.

📍 1-17-1, Namamugi, Tsurumi-ku, Yokohama-shi, Kanagawa

🚃 Namamugi Station

📞 045-503-8250

🕐 10:00 am – 5:00 pm (Depends on tour times)

🚫 Mondays (open if holiday, closed next day), New Year's holidays

- Take home some factory-limited merchandise.
- There is a craft beer pub on the premises as well.

Rainbow Bridge
is falling down...
falling down...

Photo by: HAKU/PIXTA

A winter night by the bay

Odaiba-Kaihinkoen

📷 Odaiba Kaihin Park

February 27 is the very romantic-sounding Day of Winter's Lover. This park is a popular spot for lovebirds out for a night in Odaiba. The beach, rowdy with families during the day, is veiled with a honey-sweet atmosphere at night. Sit down on the observation deck and glance out at Tokyo Bay, taking in the Rainbow Bridge and brilliant cityscape in the dark. Take someone special—here's your chance to snuggle up for warmth.

📍 1, Daiba, Minato-ku

🚉 Odaiba-Kaihinkoen Station

📞 03-5531-0852 (Odaiba Kaihin Park Management Office)

🕐 24 hours

🚫 –

• In December, the Rainbow Bridge actually glows rainbow colors.
• The park is also perfect for a jog.

Treat yourself!

Nothing lackluster here!

Ginza-itchome

🎁 Ginza Bakery

A mecca for pastry lovers in Ginza. Their signature dessert is the first come, first served Castella Biscuit Sandwich. A big, fat dollop of not-too-sweet cream sits between biscuits with a unique moist texture. Get them with raisins or without. Who knew a simple biscuit could be so profound? Even if these are sold out by the time you get there, there are plenty of other delectable desserts to choose from, so don't worry.

📍 1-5-5, Ginza, Chuo-ku

🚇 Ginza-itchome Station

📞 03-3538-0155

🕐 11:00 am – 8:00 pm
Sundays: 11:00 am – 6:00 pm

🚫 Irregular

- Their other signature dessert, G Stick Sesame, is also a must-try.
- We also recommend the Rare's Cookies.

How about some light reading by the fountain?

See the park made famous by novelist Haruki Murakami

Hibiya

🚶 Hibiya Park

On a warm, sunny day, taking a break at the edge of a fountain sounds appealing. Hibiya Park is smack in the middle of a business district, and it is where many office workers come to get a breath of fresh air during the week. On weekends, food fairs and other outdoor events fill the park with excitement. The park has also made an appearance in Haruki Murakami's novel *Hard-Boiled Wonderland and the End of the World*. Pretend you're the novel's protagonist and gulp down some beer, book in hand. Not a bad way to spend a day, right?

📍	Hibiya-koen, Chiyoda-ku
🚉	Hibiya Station
📞	03-3501-6428
🕐	24 hours
🚫	–

- In fall, there's the *Gotochi Nabe* (a local hot pot) Festival.
- In winter, come here for the Tokyo Christmas Market.

Satisfying stress release

Try this unusual date venue

Kichijoji

🚶 Shooting Bar EA

If you want to try another approach to stress relief, how about this shooting bar? Step into the longest shooting lane of Tokyo (32.8 feet), then ready your air gun. Now aim and fire! The thrill of hitting the target is addictive—you might get hooked, even if you've never been a fan of laser tag or Airsoft. Enjoy a drink while you shoot.

📍 2nd Fl. 1-5-5, Gotenyama, Musashino-shi

🚉 Kichijoji Station

📞 0422-26-9100

🕐 5:00 pm – 1:00 am
Fridays and Saturdays:
5:00 pm – 4:00 am

🚫 Tuesdays

- A variety of guns are available.
- Beginner-friendly coaches are here to guide you.

Get excited for Hinamatsuri with these!

Soft serve-shaped hina-arare *for Hinamatsuri?*

Nakameguro

🎁 Ooedo Arare Main Store

March 3 is Hinamatsuri, also known as Dolls' Day or Girls' Day. A type of rice cracker called *arare* is traditionally eaten on this day, and you'll want to pick up these two at Ooedo Arare. The first is Sakura Okaki, reminiscent of Japanese macarons. Sandwiched between the slightly salted, cherry blossom-shaped crackers is a moist, sweet, red bean paste. The other must-have is the Soft Serve Senbei. Soft-serve-shaped sugar candy covers the top of a *senbei* rice cracker. Get some for any little girls in your life—they'll love them.

📍 1-23-1-104, Kamimeguro, Meguro-ku

🚉 Nakameguro Station

📞 03-3712-4728

🕐 11:00 am – 8:00 pm
Saturdays and holidays:
11:00 am – 6:00 pm

🚫 Sundays, New Year's holidays, Golden Week, summer holidays

- You can buy the freshly made crackers from the live demonstrations on Wednesday, Thursday, and Saturday.
- The Shita Zutsumi and Ebiyose are also fantastic.

A perfect gift for all your friends

Tiny, colorful mochi for a feel of spring

Sakura-Shimmachi

🎁 Takeno to Ohagi

This *ohagi* (type of glutinous rice mochi dessert) specialty shop was heartwarmingly named after the store owner's grandmother. Aside from the red bean paste passed down from Grandma, the *ohagi* are also stuffed with seasonal fillings like pistachio, mulberry, or cherry. Pack the *ohagi* into bent-woodware boxes, and seal it with your choice of *washi* tape. These are ideal for gift giving, but you'll want some for yourself, too. These desserts will pump you up for spring in the cutest way.

📍 1-21-11 Sakurashimmachi, Setagaya-ku

🚃 Sakura-Shimmachi Station

📞 03-6413-1227

🕐 12:00 pm – 6:00 pm (or until sold out)

🚫 Mondays and Tuesdays

- Combinations like Algae Salt and Cherry and Coconut and Lemon Peel will grab your attention.
- Persimmon and Roast *Matcha* is also incredible.

A treasure hunt in a European mansion!

Photo by: THE GLOBE ANTIQUES

The antique furniture shop with a feel of Belgium

Sangenjaya

♯ The Globe Antiques

This antique shop, piled with furniture selected from countries like England or Belgium, feels like the set of a period film. There are plenty of tools and items for DIY projects, and a café attached to the first floor. Revel in this little European world to your heart's content; it's a perfect place to hunt for hidden treasures. From repairing to personalizing the furniture you've purchased, this caring antique shop has got your back.

📍 2-7-8, Ikejiri, Setagaya-ku

🚌 Sangenjaya Station

📞 03-5430-3662

🕐 11:00 am – 7:30 pm

🚫 –

- The lighting and stained glass are ridiculously seductive.
- Proper meals like roast beef are available in the café.

A destination that feels like an exotic resort

Yoyogi

✕ Yoyogi Village

Here you'll find a cluster of open terrace restaurants and cafés, scattered between the flourishing green of plants from around the world. You'd be surprised to know it's only a three-minute walk from the station, and right in the middle of the city. Come to the delicious Yoyogi Curry for lunch, and spend your evening at the posh Music Bar. Stare up at the sky in this space with the luxury to do whatever you want, however you want, whenever you want.

📍 1-28-9, Yoyogi, Shibuya-ku

🚇 Yoyogi Station

📞 03-6826-5556

🕐 Depends on the store

🚫 Depends on the store

- Events like the Scandinavian market abound.
- The regularly scheduled Garden Making workshop seems like fun.

See if you can find the secret heart stone

The sophisticated alleyway for a zen night out

Iidabashi

✕ Kagurazaka Kakurenbo Yokocho Alley

This atmospheric alleyway is lined with tasteful establishments such as restaurants converted from traditional *minka* homes, tempura restaurants over a century old, and restaurants with sunken hearths. Undeniably, the alley's main feature is its beautiful, rustic cobblestone streets. Hidden among the stones are heart-, star-, and diamond-shaped ones. Search for them and make a wish when you find one.

📍 Near 3, Kagurazaka, Shinjuku-ku

🚉 Iidabashi Station

📞 Depends on the store

🕐 Depends on the store

🚫 Depends on the store

- Take an Insta-worthy picture against the cobblestones.
- Some of the restaurants and bars are intimidatingly stylish, but don't let that put you off.

So fragrant and delicious!

Try the fatty mackerel

Daikanyama

✕ Sabar

March 8 is Mackerel Day, so head to the fatty mackerel specialty restaurant where the fish is even better than fatty tuna. Start with the Seared Fatty Mackerel Pressed Sushi, then go full out with other incredible mackerel cuisine from around the world that'll have you exclaiming, "Holy mackerel!" Try mackerel yukhoe (similar to ceviche), mackerel fish and chips, a gooey mackerel melt sandwich, or an elegant smoked mackerel salad. Hope your day is going swimmingly! This is Sabar, Ebisu branch.

📍 B1, 1-30-14, Ebisunishi, Shibuya-ku

🚃 Daikanyama Station

📞 03-6452-5238

🕐 5:00 pm – 11:38 pm

🚫 Irregular

- The Mega-Fatty Mackerel Sashimi is a must-have.
- To wrap up the night, soak the Seasoned Mackerel Rice Bowl with mackerel broth and make it an *ochazuke*.

"Best in Japan" might just be correct

Is this the best shortcake in Japan?

Sugamo

French Pound House

A shortcake served with elegant simplicity, Rouge is made with a rice-flour sponge that melts in your mouth, while the strawberry juice meringue blends refreshingly with the cream. Strawberry liquor and kirsch (fruit brandy) is also used for flavoring. Buy this cake for someone special.

- 1-4-4, Sugamo, Toshima-ku
- Sugamo Station
- 03-3944-2108
- 10:00 am – 8:00 pm
- New Year's holidays

- Blanc is the nonalcoholic version.
- Their mousse and fruit tarts are, obviously, amazing.

Mint lovers won't be able to get enough!

Mint chocolate fanatics: be there or be square

Sangenjaya

✗ Shaved Ice Café Banpaku

Banpaku operates out of a borrowed music venue during the day. Here, you can taste shaved ice made lovingly with handmade syrup and pure ice. In particular, we recommend the Mint Chocolate Shaved Ice. This unforgettable shaved ice is the definition of refreshing. Not to mention, the crackle of the chocolate is indescribable. By the way, March 10 is Mint Day.

📍 B1, 2-23-5, Taishido, Setagaya-ku

🚃 Sangenjaya Station

📞 –

🕐 12:00 pm – 6:00 pm

🚫 Irregular

- We also recommend the crimson Berry Almond Milk.
- The Honey Lemon Rare Cheese is tempting too.

Time-travel for some vintage fun

Reunite with the near-extinct penny arcade at this museum

Itabashihoncho

🚶 Dagashiya Game Museum

Feel nostalgic at the sight of penny arcade machines? Come face-to-face with the good old days at this museum. Retro Japanese penny arcade machines like *Conquest Battle* or *Rock-Paper-Scissors Man* line the space, taking you back to the '70s. Go with friends, or bring your family while touring around Tokyo.

📍 17-8, Miyamotocho, Itabashi-ku

🚃 Itabashihoncho Station

📞 —

🕐 2:00 pm – 7:00 pm
Weekends and holidays:
10:00 am – 7:00 pm

🚫 Tuesdays and Wednesdays
(open if holiday)

- The owner's video explanations of the machines are helpful.
- You could play all day with just ¥1,000 and still have change to spare.

This is what the '70s were like, huh?

Nostalgic penny candies

Shibamata

🎁 Shibamata High Color Yokocho

March 12 is *Dagashi* Day. *Dagashi* is Japanese penny candy, and you can hoard them at High Color Yokocho Alley in Shibamata, famous for being where the movie *Otoko wa Tsurai yo* and the manga *Kochira Katsushika-ku Kameari Kōen-mae Hashutsujo* are set. Thousands of types of *dagashi* are available, and you can relish the atmosphere of the swinging Japanese '70s. As you wade to the back, you'll see a corner filled with collectible photographs of stars from the era.

📍 7-3-12, Shibamata, Katsushika-ku

🚉 Shibamata Station

📞 03-3673-9627

🕐 10:00 am – 7:00 pm

🚫 Fridays (museum only open on weekends and holidays)

- The entry fee to the Toy Museum on the second floor is just ¥200.
- There are many penny arcade machines here, too.

Crap! I'm gonna buy everything!

Need to wrap a present? You've come to the right place

Nishi-Ogikubo

Red Heart Store

If you need to wrap a cute present, this is the place to go. Over 1,000 kinds of Mrs. Grossman's stickers are imported from the United States. There's a wall of Sticker Rolls in all varieties from animals to flowers to hearts. You might be transported back to your own sticker-collecting childhood as you look for the right ones to make someone happy. Just one sticker on a plain bag can make your gift wrapping original.

📍 3-21-7-101, Nishiogiminami, Suginami-ku

🚇 Nishi-Ogikubo Station

📞 03-3331-2413

🕐 12:00 pm – 6:00 pm

🚫 Sundays, Mondays, holidays (may be closed without notice)

- Sticker Art workshops are available.
- Don't forget to check out Halloween or other seasonal stickers.

A bouquet of candy is so cool!

Give someone a caramel bouquet

Asakusa

👝 Noake Tokyo

This store is key to some classy gift giving. Les Bonbons Caramel (¥2,600 for ten) is made by caramelizing fruit purée, and the treacly texture will have you hooked. It's delicious, and the bouquet-shaped packaging will no doubt make the recipient feel special. Just picture the look of joy on their face when you present them with this!

📍	5-3-7, Asakusa, Taito-ku
🚉	Asakusa Station
📞	03-5849-4256
🕐	11:00 am – 5:30 pm
🚫	Sundays and Mondays

- Print text on the sticks for ¥5 per bonbon.
- Try the summer-only Candy Frappé.

A karaoke venue perfect for spring break

Higashi-Shinjuku

🚶 Lux-Ria Tokyo

It's spring break, and you want to do something a little special? This slightly decadent karaoke venue is the answer! Located in Kabukicho, Shinjuku, the luxury, photo-ready interior of this place is unforgettable. Emotions run high as the holidays come to an end, so why not let it all out with a song or two? Trip planners looking for an after dinner activity, put this on your list.

📍 4th Fl. Sankei75 Bldg. 2-20-9, Kabukicho, Shinjuku-kku

🚃 Higashi-Shinjuku Station

📞 03-5155-1547

🕐 Reservation required: 3:00 pm – 12:00 am

🚫 –

• Three of the karaoke rooms are full of personality.
• The sound systems are A+.

Everyone's heart will skip a beat

© @home cafe

Never been to a maid café? Go on, try it

Akihabara

✕ @Home Cafe

If you're in Akihabara, try visiting a maid café, even if it's just once. Among all the available choices, @Home is exemplary. Lovely maids are eager to serve you, their master or mistress. After having the handmade omelet rice or the dreamy parfait, take a photo or play games with them. Your heart will undoubtedly skip a beat for these sweet young women.

📍 3rd to 7th Fl. 1-11-4, Sotokanda, Chiyoda-ku

🚃 Akihabara Station

📞 03-5207-9779

🕐 11:00 am – 10:00 pm
Weekends and holidays:
10:00 am – 10:00 pm

🚫 –

- Watch as a maid shakes a Mixed Juice before your eyes.
- On your birthday, festivities are free.

The artistic cup is so cute!

The coffee stand in the heart of Shibuya

Yoyogi-Koen

✕ The Latte Tokyo

To get to know the heart of busy Shibuya, known as Oku-Shibuya, a little better, start with the concept store Inn. Within just 131.6 square feet of space, the shop features the coffee stand The Latte Tokyo, fashion brand Post Amenities, and even limited pop-up shops. Keep an eye out for the stylish artist collaboration cups, as the designs change regularly.

📍 101, 3-3, Kamiyamacho, Shibuya-ku

🚇 Yoyogi-Koen Station

📞 03-6416-8298

🕐 8:00 am – 7:00 pm
Weekends and holidays:
10:00 am – 6:00 pm

🚫 Irregular

- Their signature is Tokyo Latte, which uses Tokyo Milk.
- Plenty of flavored latte choices are available, too.

Doing nothing is a luxury in itself

Photo by: Oku

Anime fans will enjoy scene spotting here

Shinjuku-Gyoenmae

🚶 Shinjuku Gyoen

You can get to Shinjuku Gyoen in ten minutes on foot from Shinjuku Station. This is a tranquil park full of nature, with over ten thousand flourishing trees. When the spring breeze is warm, pull out a picnic blanket, lie back and relax. Stare up at the sky as the sun warms you and feel your fatigue vanishing. At the in-park restaurant, you can try the dessert set made with vegetables from traditional Edo cuisine, including a burdock gateau-chocolat and mustard-spinach pound cake.

📍 11, Naitomachi, Shinjuku-ku

🚃 Shinjuku-Gyoenmae Station

📞 03-3350-0151

🕐 9:00 am – 4:30 pm

🚫 Mondays (open if holiday, closed next business day)

- Sit on the bench that appeared in Shinkai Makoto's animated film, *The Garden of Words*.
- Alcohol and toys are forbidden on the premises.

March

19

15-minute shows are just the right length

Photo by: Tokyo International Air Terminal

A planetarium café in an airport

Haneda Airport International Terminal

🚶 Planetarium Starry Café

This café is worth going all the way to the airport for. This spot, inside Haneda Airport, is no ordinary coffee shop; it's also a planetarium that lets you stargaze while you eat. After paying the entrance fee (¥520, plus one mandatory drink order), move to the dome in the back, where you are free to enjoy fifteen-minute planetarium programs to your heart's content. With star-themed cocktails in one hand, relax and experience the universe. Drop in before your flight out of Tokyo.

📍 5th Fl. Haneda Airport International Terminal, Ota-ku

🚉 Haneda Airport International Terminal Station

📞 03-6428-0694

🕐 7:00 am – 11:00 pm

🚫 –

- Order a hot dog—you'll feel like you're at the movies.
- Check out some planes from the observation deck before you leave.

This looks like a set for a movie!

The heart-shaped waterfall

Kazusa-Kameyama

📷 Kameiwa Cave

This scenic valley is very popular on social media. Also known as Noumizo Falls, the waterfall and the curtain of light flooding into the cave looks simply otherworldly. In the early mornings, the reflection of the light on the water creates the Heart Waterfall. The best time to catch this sight is March or September, but between June and early July, it's worth camping out until evening to catch a glimpse of fireflies in this mystical space. Anyone would feel rejuvenated just strolling along the tree-cocooned walkways.

📍 1954, Sasa, Kimitsu-shi, Chiba

🚉 Kazusa-Kameyama Station and on-demand taxi (reservation required)

📞 0439-56-1325 (Kimitsu Ward Office Tourism Department)

🕐 24 hours

🚫 –

- Stop by the hole-in-the-wall Senju Hot Springs nearby.
- Pick up some fresh local produce at the station before leaving.

Strawberry heaven

Spring day trip? It's gotta be strawberry-picking!

Koshigaya

🚶 Koshigaya Strawberry Town

The spring equinox is here, so choose a time to come out for a day of nonstop strawberries. As you enter the greenhouse you'll be overwhelmed by their sweet fragrance. Grown in an unbelievably nature-rich environment only one hour out of Tokyo, these sweet berries are so delicious you'll be beaming after just one bite. Pick as many as you like, and savor them to your heart's content.

📍 1-41, Mashimori, Koshigaya-shi, Saitama

🚆 Koshigaya Station and bus

📞 048-965-1514

🕐 Weekdays start from 10:00 am
Weekends and holidays by reservation from 10:00 am and 11:30 am
Note: Closes when the strawberries run out

🚫 Jan. to Feb.: Mondays and Fridays
Mar. 1 to May 6: Mondays
Closed from May 7

• The stories about honey bees are interesting.
• Different strawberry cultivars like the "benihoppe," "akihime," and "kaorino" are all-you-can-eat!

Even better than cheese

Japanese fondue with bittersweet matcha chocolate

Ushigome-Kagurazaka

✗ Kagurazaka Saryo

This is a dessert you'll want in your mouth as soon as you hear its name: Bittersweet *Matcha* and White Chocolate Hot Japanese-Style Chocolate Fondue. Doesn't it sound amazing? Dip *shiratama* dumplings or strawberries into that rich chocolate sauce and tuck in, then polish off the last of the sauce by pouring it over vanilla ice cream. This is definitely what happiness tastes like. Now that it feels like spring outside, enjoy your desserts on the relaxing terrace seats.

📍 5-9, Kagurazaka, Shinjuku-ku

🚇 Ushigome-Kagurazaka Station

📞 03-3266-0880

🕐 11:30 am – 11:00 pm
Sundays and holidays:
11:30 – 10:00 pm

🚫 Irregular

- Try their premium selection of Japanese and Chinese teas.
- For lunch, we suggest their udon noodles and porridge.

The epitome of spring in Japan

Photo by: kazu-ab/PIXTA

All aboard for fields of canola blossoms

Moka

📷 Moka Railway

Constructed in 1912, the Moka Railway is Japan's first local railway. It runs for twenty-six miles between Shimodate Station in Ibaraki and Motegi Station in Tochigi. The highlight is, without a doubt, the combination of canola blossoms, cherry blossoms, and the train. Picture a colorful train charging through a pink tunnel of cherry blossoms on a rug of yellow canola blossoms laid over the train tracks. Catching this flower-gazing train, which runs at a leisurely pace of 17.3 miles an hour, is the best way to see this extraordinary sight.

📍 2474-1, Daimachi, Moka-shi, Tochigi

🚉 Moka Station

📞 0285-84-2911

🕐 Check website

🚫 —

- Black steam locomotives also use these tracks.
- Enjoy the Steam Locomotive Lunch Box on the train.

Supernatural
Japanese beings
in edible form

Too cute to eat! Come here for the most charming daifuku

Nippori

🎁 Edo Usagi

This is the famous Yokai Apricot *Daifuku*. *Daifuku* is a powdered mochi stuffed with sweet fillings, often red bean paste or fruit. This *daifuku* has beady black eyes of sesame and a whole apricot sticking out. It looks like a *yokai* (supernatural being) chomping down on fruit, and it's just too adorable. With their charming design and fantastic flavors, they're often sold out before noon. There are fillings such as red bean paste and milk paste, as well as other fruit stuffings like strawberry and chestnut.

📍 2-14-11, Nishi-Nippori, Arakawa-ku

🚇 Nippori Station

📞 03-3891-1432

🕐 9:00 am – 6:00 pm
(Open until 5:30 pm in winter)

🚫 Sundays, holidays, irregular days

- The closed-mouth Mizu-Manju is precious, as well.
- An eat-in space beside the store is available if you'd like to sit down.

This might be perfect for some alone time

Enjoy the classical music streaming from the amplifiers

Asagaya

🚶 Violon

This music café sits quietly in a tranquil residential area. This is a space to serenely enjoy your coffee while listening to the classical music coming from the towering speakers in the back of the shop. It's not a great space to converse, but it's ideal for reading a book or untangling your thoughts. It's almost a new season, so sink into the sofas and think about all the places you've seen and fallen in love with in Tokyo.

📍 2-9-5, Asagayakita, Suginami-ku

🚆 Asagaya Station

📞 03-3336-6414

🕐 Recordings played:
12:00 pm – 6:00 pm
Live music from 6:00 pm
Note: Performances start and end depending on the program

🚫 Tuesdays

- Have a homemade cheesecake with the coffee.
- Check out the giant gramophone, too.

A spectacular view!

Photo by: soooo.ta

A view of Mount Fuji, Skytree, and Mount Tsukuba, too

Funabori

📷 Tower Hall Funabori

Here's something to make your trip even more special. Visit the free-to-enter Funabori Tower, located by the Arakawa River in the Edogawa Ward. The massive, 360-degree panorama of the city gives you a sweeping view of everything from Mount Fuji to Tokyo Skytree, all the way to Mount Tsukuba. Now that you're here, you can proudly say you've seen all of Tokyo.

📍 4-1-1, Funabori, Edogawa-ku

🚆 Funabori Station

📞 03-5676-2211

🕘 9:00 am – 9:30 pm

🚫 Elevator operation may be suspended depending on weather conditions

- You may catch a glimpse of Diamond Fuji in November or February.
- You'll find a movie theater on the lower floors.

Photo by: ytbcraft

Enjoy cherry blossoms on a boat, just the two of you

Hanzomon

🚶 Chidorigafuchi Moat

With April just around the corner, March 27 is Cherry Day. Go blossom-viewing in one of the best spots in Tokyo. The banks around the moat are adorned with over 260 cherry varieties such as the *somei-yoshino* cherry and oriental cherry. The drooping branches in full bloom are alluring, ephemeral, and just a little wistful. Maybe you'll even see a little bit of yourself in the blossoms that come after enduring a hard winter. How do the cherry blossoms look to you?

📍	From 2 Kudanshita to 3bancho, Chiyoda-ku
🚇	Hanzomon Station
📞	03-3556-0391 (Chiyoda Ward Tourism Association)
🕐	Illumination from around 6:00 pm until 10:00 pm
🚫	–

- The Cherry Blossom Festival is held between late March and early April.
- There are illuminations at night.

A little getaway!

Photo by: Shinta/PIXTA

Ten minutes from the station, a verdant vista to calm your soul

Higashi-Kurume

Chikurin Park

In Tokyo, there's a bamboo forest reminiscent of Kyoto's famous Arashiyama. Chosen as one of the One Hundred Views of New Tokyo, you can be showered in green in this park of over two thousand bamboo trees. The sweet aroma of bamboo, the comforting sound of leaves rustling in the wind... If it's been a while since you stargazed, stretch your arms out, take a deep breath, and feel the excess tension leave your body. Who knew such a rejuvenating place existed just ten minutes from the station?

- 1-7, Minamisawa, Higashikurume-shi
- Higashi-Kurume Station
- 042-470-7753 (Higashikurume Environment Policy Department)
- 24 hours
- –

- Bring some hot coffee in a bottle, and take a break.
- Look up and take a photo of the sunlight filtering through the bamboo.

Spring has come again

A view so beautiful, it's sobering

Roppongi

📷 Midtown Blossom

There's no place better than Tokyo to enjoy the contrast between the cityscape and the proliferation of cherry blossoms. Tokyo Midtown's cherry blossom street is illuminated at night, highlighting the to-die-for scenery. It's so beautiful you might be afraid to get used to it. A perfect place to think, dream or meditate.

📍 9-7-1, Akasaka, Minato-ku

🚇 Roppongi Station

📞 03-3475-3100
(10:00 am – 9:00 pm)

🕐 Shops: 11:00 am – 9:00 pm
Restaurants: 11:00 am – 12:00 am

🚫 –

- Take in the sight of lit-up cherry blossoms and Tokyo Tower together.
- On the garden terrace, have some champagne while enjoying the view.

There's something lovely about lanterns

Locals and tourists alike will enjoy this atmospheric alleyway

Shibuya

✗ Shibuya Nonbei Yokocho

Some of the charming remnants of postwar Tokyo nestle here in the heart of the concrete jungle. Here, at Drunkard's Alley, (*nonbei yokocho*) you'll find cheerful bartenders who whip up family-style cuisine, grilled chicken specialty restaurants, even hole-in-the-wall bars. Tokyo is glamorous neon lights, but it's also alleyways lit by red lanterns. Drink while the sun's out, or quietly by yourself. A peaceful spot for a quiet drink whether you're a local or a visitor.

📍 1-25-9 to 1-25-10, Shibuya, Shibuya-ku

🚌 Shibuya Station

📞 Depends on the store

🕐 Depends on the store

🚫 Depends on the store

- Over thirty unique bars and restaurants are squeezed tightly into the alley.
- The lanterns are photo worthy all on their own.

There's still plenty to discover

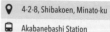

Tokyo Tower is waiting for you

Akabanebashi

Tokyo Tower

No matter which new buildings go up, the Symbol of Tokyo never changes. It has a different meaning for everyone: people who come to visit, those who were born nearby, people who stare up at it as they go about their lives. Tokyo Tower holds many memories, but this red, 1,092.5-foot-tall tower has always welcomed people to Tokyo and always will.

📍 4-2-8, Shibakoen, Minato-ku

🚇 Akabanebashi Station

📞 03-3433-5111

🕐 Main Deck (492 ft):
9:00 am – 10:30 pm

🚫 –

• Between 11:00 am and 4:00 pm (excluding rainy days) on weekends and holidays, the outdoor stairs are open.
• A good place to bring your parents if they're traveling with you.

Champagne and good vibes

Photo by: genki/PIXTA

Celebrate spring with this sightseeing staple

Nakameguro

📷 Cherry Blossom Festival

The best view of cherry blossoms in Tokyo? Undoubtedly the Meguro River. When it's covered by an exquisite pink blanket of fallen petals from over eight hundred cherry trees, the view of this river is one of the most unforgettable sights of Tokyo. At night, the colors are enriched by the flickering city lights. The Cherry Blossom Festival occurs between late March and early April, and there is an abundance of food stalls for your browsing and eating pleasure.

📍 Meguro-ku, along the Meguro River

🚇 Nakameguro Station

📞 –

🕐 Illuminations between 5:00 pm – 9:00 pm

🚫 –

- Snap a pic of the cherry-colored river!
- The Meguro River Cherry-Blossom Cruise (from ¥3,900) is worth it.

Cute donuts and great coffee

Grab coffee and donuts to go!

Hiroo

✗ Canvas Tokyo

An open concept store consisting of three different stores, Canvas Tokyo offers customers delicious donuts from Nico Donuts, specialty coffee from Mark Espresso, and burgers and smoothies from Ramey Circus. Situated in trendy Hiroo, this cozy, minimalist-design café is the perfect place to unwind after a day of sightseeing. Sip on an espresso or settle for a pulled pork burger. For art enthusiasts, Canvas Tokyo offers its own artist-in-residence space where it hosts pop-up stores, photo shoots, and art exhibitions.

📍 5-19-6, Hiroo, Shibuya-ku

🚇 Hiroo Station

📞 03-6432-5700

🕐 8:45 am – 6:00 pm

🚫 –

• Specialty coffee with beautiful latte art by baristas.
• A range of affordable, tasty food and drink options.

Looks and tastes like a melon!

Pretty desserts and old-school appeal

Yurakucho

✗ Bridge

Tokyo's charm goes beyond just the new and shiny. If you enjoy a vintage atmosphere, try this café, which has been here since 1958. The enticing Melon Pancake (approx. ¥1,600 for the set) is a specialty. Chunks of freshly chopped melon are sandwiched between three layers of pancake, coated with an emerald-green melon cream, and topped with a web of whipped cream. This luxurious dessert belongs in both your belly and your photo album.

📍 B1, 4-1 Ginza, Chuo-ku

🚉 Yurakucho Station

📞 03-3566-4081

🕐 11:00 am - 8:30 pm
Sundays and holidays:
11:00 am - 8:00 pm

🚫 In accordance with Nishiginza
(shopping mall where it is located)

• The Snow White Pancake is super refreshing.
• The hamburger steaks and other savory items are great, too.

Look at these jewel-like appetizers!

Enjoy runway-worthy Italian fashion while you eat

Meguro

✗ Rinascimento

Feeling like some sophisticated Italian? Try Rinascimento, where you can dig into the unforgettable appetizer, Insaratissima Rinascimento. Thirty different bite-sized appetizers are presented like a work of art. You'll want to take your time savoring each one. The interior and tableware express the place's abundant individuality, delivering a unique experience. Lunch starts from ¥2,700.

📍 1st Fl. 2-23-2, Shimomeguro, Meguro-ku

🚃 Meguro Station

📞 03-6420-3623

🕐 12:00 pm – 1:30 pm (last order)
6:00 pm – 9:30 pm (last order)

🚫 Sundays, Monday lunchtime

- You can't go wrong with the sommelier's wine recommendation.
- The option that includes more than forty types of veggies sounds good too!

Everything starts with the right tools, right?

Time to sharpen up

Ningyocho

☗ Ubukeya

This traditional blade-tool business has been around for 230 years! The name comes from *ubuke*, the Japanese word for peach fuzz or downy hair, as they once specialized in blades for shaving or cutting baby hair. You can find over three hundred types of blade-edged tools, from kitchen knives to scissors to tweezers, and almost all of them are handcrafted. Their most popular tweezers even come in four different shapes for different purposes. Spring is a time for new beginnings, so this is a good opportunity to grab the tools you need.

📍 3-9-2, Ningyocho, Nihonbashi, Chuo-ku

🚇 Ningyocho Station

📞 03-3661-4851

🕐 9:00 am – 6:00 pm
Saturdays: 9:00 am – 5:00 pm

🚫 Sundays and public holidays

- You need a new kitchen knife, you know you do.
- Sharpening service is provided (excluding nail clippers and nail files).

Anti-static
hairbrushes here

Three thousand brushes to choose from

Kodenmacho

🎁 Edoya

Here's another place that will take your quality of life up a notch. This brush specialty shop has been in business since the Edo period (16th to 18th century). Brushes for clothes, for hair, for makeup, even toothbrushes, all lovingly handmade by craftsmen. And they've got over three thousand types for you to choose from! You'll want one for every need around the house. Premium hairbrushes start from ¥2,700. Try one and find out why people keep going back for them.

📍 2-16, Odenmacho, Nihonbashi, Chuo-ku

🚉 Kodenmacho Station

📞 03-3664-5671

🕘 9:00 am – 5:00 pm

🚫 Weekends and holidays

- Pick up a brush for cleaning the washroom or kitchen.
- Suitcase full? Grab another from their online shop.

Now THIS is cherry blossom viewing in Tokyo

Photo by: Alan/PIXTA

A perfect photo opportunity

Asakusa

📷 Cherry Blossom Viewing

Sumida River is famous for its cherry blossoms. Find the perfect place for a shot of Skytree Tower framed by flowers. Sumida River is lined with cherry trees on both sides for well over a half a mile, but this photo opportunity is only possible from the Taito Ward side. The Bokutei Cherry Blossom Festival and the Sumida Park Cherry Blossom Festival are hosted annually. After sunset, you can enjoy a gorgeous night view of the blossoms illuminated by paper lanterns, with traditional Japanese houseboats adrift in the river behind them.

📍 Near 7-1, Asakusa, Taito-ku
Near 1, Mukojima, Sumida-ku

🚉 Asakusa Station

📞 –

🕐 All hours

🚫 –

• The festivals take place from late March to early April.
• Keep an eye out for Skytree's seasonal illuminations.

Night-lit cherry blossoms 250 meters above the ground

Toranomon

Andaz Tokyo

If you're looking for a metropolitan cherry blossom viewing experience exclusive to Tokyo, the Rooftop Bar at Andaz Tokyo is it. The seasonal Cherry Blossom Garden is a cherry tree-filled terrace 820 feet above ground. At night, stare up at the blossoms, and down at the illuminated Tokyo Tower with their Night Blossom Dinner, and enjoy their Blossom Viewing Afternoon Tea during the day. Come on in to this garden in the sky!

- 1-23-4, Toranomon, Minato-ku
- Toranomon Station
- 03-6830-7739 (restaurant reservation line)
- Check-in: 3:00 pm
  Check-out: 12:00 pm
- –

- Open during peak cherry blossom season.
- Don't miss the night view from the top of Toranomon Hills.

Almost too cute to eat

Twenty-four miniature sushi—try them all

Shinsen

✗ Maruyamacho Wadatsumi

If you want sushi in Tokyo, you must go here. The must-have lunch Hime Nigiri (¥2,000, reservation required) is a platter of thumb-sized *edomaezushi*—traditionally made sushi using fish or shellfish from Tokyo Bay. These bite-size, authentically prepared morsels are made with fresh seasonal fish and allow you to try all twenty-four types of sushi without running out of room. With its corridors and closed rooms, you almost forget you're in Shibuya when you step into the world of Wadatsumi.

📍 6-1, Maruyamacho, Shibuya-ku

🚉 Shinsen Station

📞 03-6455-0267

🕐 12:00 pm – 2:30 pm
6:00 pm – 11:30 pm

🚫 Sundays and holidays

• Splurge a little on the *kaiseki*, the traditional multicourse Japanese dinner (from ¥7,000).
• A great place to bring a loved one for their birthday.

Sea urchin on top of meat!?

Must-try sea urchin and beef roll

Iidabashi

✕ Tobiushi

In this *yakiniku* (Japanese-style barbecue) restaurant, you can savor top-shelf Japanese *wagyu* in private rooms. The first dish you must try is the Sea Urchin Beef Roll (¥1,300). Beautifully marbled Japanese A5 *wagyu* is wrapped around a bite-size rice ball, and an ample serving of sea urchin sits on top. It melts into a harmony of flavors in your mouth; drizzle some sweet Kyushu soy sauce over it and dig in! Other original creations like *Heremeshi*—thickly sliced tenderloin served boldly and simply on rice—are also waiting for you.

📍	4th and 5th Fl. 2-2-12, Fujimi, Chiyoda-ku
🚉	Iidabashi Station
📞	050-7534-0752
🕐	5:00 pm – 11:00 pm
🚫	Mondays, New Year's holidays

• Try the Foie Gras Sushi.
• And the Tobiushi Roast Yukhoe.

Just like the bed forts you used to build!

Read till you fall asleep in a bookstore-hotel

Ikebukuro

⬛ Book and Bed Tokyo

You're in Tokyo and a standard hotel just won't cut it. If you're a hard-core bookworm, how about a bookstore you can spend the night in? Crawl into the bed space behind the shelves and enjoy the book buffet of novels, manga, and magazines. Pile up books next to your pillow and drift off reading while snuggled into the fluffy duvet. Book lovers dream of ending the night like this; here, it's reality.

📍 7th Fl. 1-17-7, Nishiikebukuro, Toshima-ku

🚌 Ikebukuro Station

📞 –

🕐 Check-in: 4:00 pm
Check-out: 11:00 am
Daytime operation:
1:00 pm – 5:00 pm

🚫 Daytime operations may be suspended for events or interviews

- In the Asakusa location, there are rooms for two.
- Pajama rentals are available.

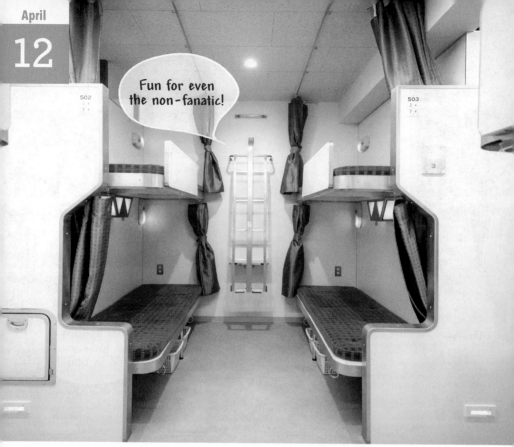

R.project Inc.

A hostel built from reclaimed trains

Bakurocho

🏨 Train Hostel Hokutosei

When Hokutosei, the sleeping car train service that ran from Ueno, Tokyo, to Sapporo, Hokkaido was discontinued, there was a public outcry. But it has been reborn as a hostel using original parts from the train, evoking a sense of nostalgia for its "passengers." Hungry? Head to the dining hall, a beautiful replica of the Grand Chariot, the dining car from Hokutosei. With reasonable prices and direct access from Bakurocho station, this is a great way to elevate your Tokyo experience!

📍 1-10-12, Bakurocho, Nihonbashi, Chuo-ku

🚆 Bakurocho Station

📞 03-6661-1068

🕐 Check-in: 4:00 pm – 11:00 pm
Check-out: 11:00 am

🚫 –

- Semiprivate rooms with desk and chair are available.
- The shared kitchen is free to use.

These movie cocktails take you back

Cocktails inspired by your favorite film

Shibuya

✗ The Whales of August

If you're looking for a late night out in Tokyo, this bar is the place to go. A little way out of the bustle of Shibuya is The Whales of August (*Hachigatsu no Kujira*), where every item on the menu is named after a movie. The cocktail pictured is Beauty and the Beast. Look at the size of that dragon fruit and those pineapples! They're really not holding back here. Other famous drinks include Hairspray and Rapunzel. Ask the bartender for your favorite movie!

📍 B1, 2nd Fl. 28-13, Udagawacho, Shibuya-ku

🚉 Shibuya Station

📞 03-3476-7238

🕐 6:00 pm – 4:00 am

🚫 Irregular

• Only movie-inspired bartender-created cocktails are available.

April

14

> What comes after happily ever after? That's up to you!

Drink with the fairies

Higashi-Ginza

✕ Tír na nÓg

Hidden in the heart of Ginza, Tokyo's renowned shopping district, there is a building with a heavy iron door, and behind that door is a bar where fae reside. Dimly lit and otherworldly, this place is like a dark fairy tale. You'll want to try the white rum-based drink, Heaven Lonely Flows. Wrapped in a whorl of wispy cotton candy, it looks like a fairy in flight. Raise your glasses, for we flirt with the ethereal tonight!

📍 B1, 5-9-5, Ginza, Chuo-ku

🚉 Higashi-Ginza Station

📞 03-6274-6416

🕐 7:00 pm – 4:00 am
Sundays: 6:00 pm – 11:30 pm

🚫 Irregular (call first)

- Keep an eye out for decor like taxidermy butterflies.
- Cover charge applies.

土木展

DOBOKU
Civil Engineering
土木工

つなぐ
なが
す
ほ
る
た
める

21_21 DESIGN SIGHT 企画展　西村 浩ディレクション「土木展」
2016.6.24（金）>>> 9.25（日）
開館時間：10:00-19:00（入場は18:30まで）　休館日：火曜日
※8月23日（火）は17:00閉館（最終入場は16:30）

21_21 DESIGN SIGHT Exhibition "DOBOKU: Civil Engineering" Directed by Hiroshi Nishimura
2016.6.24(Fri) - 9.25 (Sun) Opening Hours :10:00-19:00 (Entrance until 18:30)
Closed on Tuesdays (Except August 23)
Special opening hours for August 23 (Tue) 10:00-17:00 (Entrance until 16:30)

21_21 DESIGN SIGHT

21_21

Wonder
what's on
show?

21_21 DESIGN SIGHT (Doboku Exhibition, 2016) Roppongi

New to Tokyo's art scene? Start here

Roppongi

🚶 21_21 DESIGN SIGHT

This exhibition space is like a theme park of design. Here, you'll find exhibitions such as the Doboku Exhibition, pictured, or NHK Educational TV's Design Ah! Exhibition. But their main focus is exhibitions featuring objects and themes found in our everyday lives, such as rice, chocolate, water, and even units of measurement. Even for art novices, these events are full of fun. Go in with the intention to not just see, but to experience.

📍 9-7-6, Akasaka, Minato-ku

🚆 Roppongi Station

📞 03-3475-2121

🕐 10:00 am – 7:00 pm

🚫 Tuesdays, New Year's holidays, and between exhibitions

- 21_21 is pronounced "two-one two-one."
- Each exhibition lasts about three months.

I feel inspired already!

A gallery of constant surprises

Meiji-Jingumae <Harajuku>

🚶 Design Festa Gallery

Next, a gallery converted from an old apartment building. Before you enter, take a photo of the unique, sculpture-covered exterior. Inside, art covers more than just the gallery space—it's in the hallways, on the walls, and even in the washrooms. The gallery's events showcase a highly diverse range of art and artists. Past shows include themes such as cats, disposable cameras, girls, and the microscopic. Well worth a detour.

📍 3-20-18, Jingumae, Shibuya-ku

🚇 Meiji-Jingumae <Harajuku> Station

📞 03-3479-1442

🕐 11:00 am – 8:00 pm

🚫 During Design Festa and New Year's holidays (Dec. 30 to Jan. 3)

- Some of the art on show is available for purchase.
- Exhibition spaces start as low as ¥540.

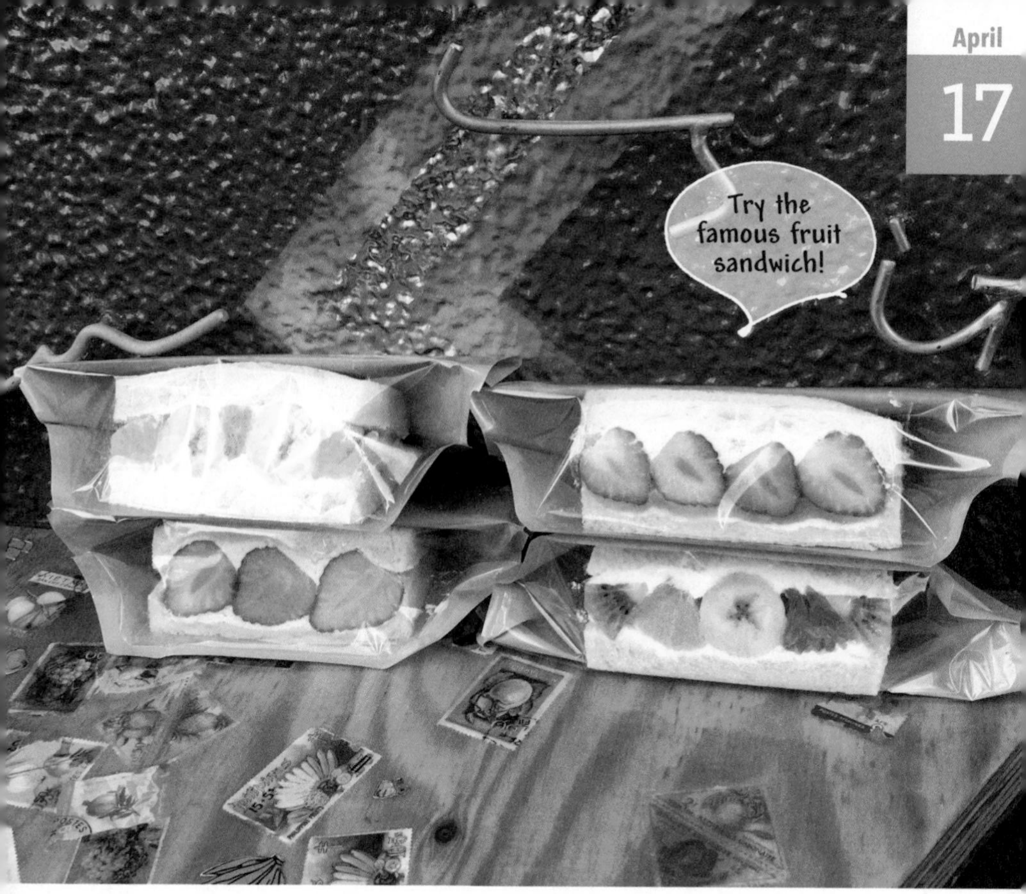
Try the
famous fruit
sandwich!

Grab a sandwich before they run out

Nakameguro

Futsuunifuruutsu

A sandwich shop so popular, the line for their sandwiches starts in one district (Nakameguro) and ends in another (Daikanyama). So do as the locals do and line up now! The shop's name comes from its signature dish, a fruit sandwich stuffed with chunks of seasonal fruit (from ¥350). The secret to their ridiculously delicious whipped cream is cane sugar and mascarpone. The heavenly combination of fluffy bread, rich cream, and fresh fruit will keep your taste buds happy. With one of these in hand, you're all set to explore Daikanyama and Meguro River.

- 1-1-71, Nakameguro, Meguro-ku
- Nakameguro Station
- 03-6451-0178
- 10:00 am – 6:00 pm
- –

- Look for the "2two22√s" sign.
- If you want to sit to eat your sandwich, the nearby coffee stand Perch has seating.

Get a message from the Tea Prince!

Royal milk tea flavored soft-serve parfait

Kitasando

✗ Tea Stand...7

If you're wandering between Sendagaya and Kitasando, drop into this specialty tea shop. The adorable pink exterior draws you right in. The Tea Prince is recommended, of course, but you must try the super-cute Pop Tea Parfait (¥780), too. After taking a photo with the storefront, put everything down and enjoy your dessert—it's so good, you'll need to concentrate.

📍 3-14-3, Sendagaya, Shibuya-ku

🚇 Kitasando Station

📞 03-5413-0578

🕐 11:00 am – 7:00 pm
Weekends and holidays:
11:00 am – 6:00 pm

🚫 Irregular

• Look out for the tea of the month.
• Check under the cup for a wholesome message.

Back-to-back movies are a real luxury

The double-feature feature of Tokyo

Meguro

🚶 Meguro Cinema

If you're gonna see a movie in Tokyo, do it in this vintage theatre. Around since 1955, this cinema has stood the test of time thanks to several renovations. One entry ticket (¥1,500 for adults) gives you access to one carefully selected double feature. Japanese, foreign-language, Hollywood, indie—the wide selection of films means there's something for everyone. Here's to stumbling across movies that change your life for the better.

📍 B1, 2-24-15, Kamiosaki, Shinagawa-ku

🚉 Meguro Station

📞 03-3491-2557

🕐 Depends on showtimes

🚫 –

- Catch the nostalgic bell before the features.
- Books on film are available for loan.

There are wineries in Tokyo!

Take the subway to a tiny urban winery

Monzennakacho

🎁 Fukagawa Winery Tokyo

Did you know that there is a winery right in Tokyo? This winery hand selects its grapes, and the entire winemaking process happens in-house. They only make thirty thousand bottles annually, and you can taste and purchase them right here. They offer a hands-on experience perfect for people looking for unique wedding favors or a special bottle for their parents. Wine lovers won't be able to get enough of this place.

📍 1-4-10, Furuishiba, Koto-ku

🚃 Monzennakacho Station

📞 03-5809-8058

🕐 Mondays and Tuesdays:
10:00 am – 6:00 pm
Wednesdays to Sundays, holidays:
10:00 am – 9:30 pm

🚫 Irregular

• The bar opens at 5 pm.
• Winery tours start at 1 pm and 3 pm on weekends and holidays (reservation required).

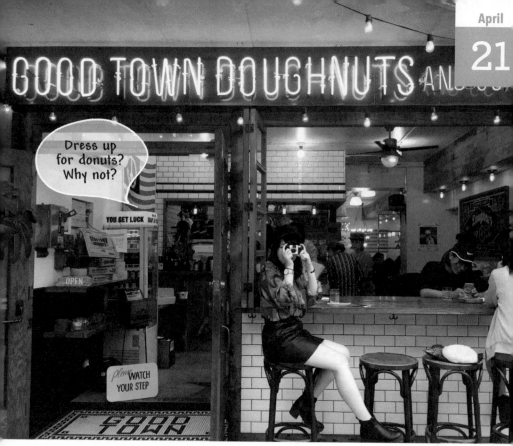

Photo by: ymo27____

Store, photogenic. Donuts, photogenic. Takeout box, photogenic!

Meiji-Jingumae <Harajuku>

✗ Good Town Doughnuts

The weather is great and nobody wants to stay cooped up at home. On these kinds of days, this gourmet takeout is where you should go. Follow the neon lights and walk up to the wooden showcase, where you'll find fluffy, chewy, delightful donuts like the aptly named Smile Mango (¥420). Get them to go in the stylish takeout box, and off you go to Yoyogi Park. It's picnic time!

📍 1st Fl. 6-12-6, Jingumae, Shibuya-ku

🚇 Meiji-Jingumae <Harajuku> Station

📞 03-5485-8827

🕐 10:00 am – 8:00 pm

🚫 –

• The most photogenic spot is in the counter seats.
• Panini and granola available for eat-in.

Experience the streets of America … in Tokyo

Ushihama

🎁 Fussa Base Side Street

Is this the USA? Are we even in Japan right now? A merge of two cultures happens here, at the edge of the Yokota Air Base. This town is made of strangely stylish antique shops, music venues, secondhand shops, art galleries, taco stands, ice cream shops—and it's all American, baby. You could point your camera anywhere, and you're still guaranteed a great shot. No passport? No problem! Welcome to "America."

📍 Along Highway 16, Fussa, Fussa-shi

🚃 Ushihama Station

📞 042-513-0432
(Fussa American House)

🕐 Depends on store

🚫 Depends on store

• Take a tour of the historic American House.
• Find the newest American street fashion in Lieon Share.

Wonder what nemophila ice cream tastes like?

Photo by: Hitachi Seaside Park

A blue world two hours away from Tokyo

Katsuta

📷 Hitachi Seaside Park

Between April and May, a bucket list–worthy "Field of Blue" appears in Ibaraki. Quilted in over 4.5 million nemophila flowers, the hill practically melts into the sky where they touch. Climb to the top, and you can look down at the cerulean Pacific. Sky, flower, sea: three majestic blue kingdoms are waiting for you, and it'll only cost you ¥450 to see them. Just two hours out from Tokyo, a day trip will give you plenty of time at the park.

📍 605-4 Onuma-aza, Mawatari, Hitachinaka-shi, Ibaraki

🚌 Katsuta Station and bus

📞 029-265-9001

🕐 9:30 am – 5:00 pm
(7 days a week, but subject to seasonal change)

🚫 Mondays (open if holiday, closed following day), New Year's holidays, first Tuesday to Friday of February

- Try the nemophila soft serve.
- Come back in fall for a crimson sea of summer cypress.

Who knew Tokyo had a spot like this!

Stay for tea in a world-class hotel

Edogawabashi

Hotel Chinzanso Tokyo

Travelers come from all around the globe to spend the night at the world-famous Hotel Chinzanso. Its enormous garden, large enough to house several historic buildings, is part of its charm. Tallest of them all, the three-storied pagoda is a must-see. Seasonal delights like the twenty types of cherry trees that blossom in spring, the fireflies of summer, and the fall foliage keep travelers coming back. Treat yourself—Chinzanso facilities like the spa and the restaurants provide service like no other.

📍 2-10-8, Sekiguchi, Bunkyo-ku

🚃 Edogawabashi Station

📞 03-3943-1111 (Representative)

🕐 Depends on facility

🚫 Depends on facility

• Staying or dining at the hotel gives you the chance to explore.
• Choose from a number of restaurants, lounges, and bars.

It's trufflicious!

Photo by: #Tsutsui's Quick Dishes

The luxurious Truffle Egg on Rice

Azabujuban

✗ Jubanukyo

"The egg on rice of all egg on rice" is right here in Tokyo, and it's called Truffles Egg on Rice (¥1,860). "How are they still in business?!" you'll exclaim as they slice you a mountain of truffles right before your eyes. The combination of fragrant truffle and rich egg yolk is so full of flavor, you won't even reach for the soy sauce. Furthermore, toppings like sea urchin and caviar can be ordered on the side! Treat yourself today for the energy to keep going tomorrow.

📍 B1F, 2-8-8, Azabujuban, Minato-ku

🚇 Azabujuban Station

📞 03-6804-6646

🕐 5:00 pm – 2:00 am
Fridays, Saturdays, days before holidays: 5:00 pm – 4:00 am
Sundays: 5:00 pm – 11:30 pm

🚫 New Year's holidays

• The "everything" in With Everything means salmon roe, sea urchin, and caviar.
• Fall for the 250 types of sake available, too.

Feel like a Tokyo connoisseur

An exquisite Sudachi Soba in a hole in the wall

Ikejiri-Ohashi

✗ Tokyo Dosanjin

Nestled in a modern building along the Meguro River, Tokyo Dosanjin is a soba noodle specialty restaurant. Their must-try dish is the Sudachi Soba. Thin slices of *sudachi*, a citrus native to Japan, float in the bowl like delicate flower petals. It may look pretty, but that's not the only thing bringing everyone back for more. Dosanjin has three types of soba noodles of different grinds, width, and thickness for you to choose from. Chic sofas in a traditional soba shop is unexpectedly novel, making Dosanjin a perfect date spot.

📍 3-19-8, Aobadai, Meguro-ku

🚃 Ikejiri-Ohashi Station

📞 03-6427-7759

🕐 11:30 am – 3:00 pm
6:00 pm – 11:00 pm

🚫 Mondays, first and third
Tuesdays of the month

- In summer, try the refreshing chilled version of their *sudachi* soba.
- The tempura and egg rolls are popular, too.

ワイルドカレーポテト

CURRY POTATO

カレー
ポテトサラダ
人参スライス
フライドガーリック
グリーンカール

500

ツナ&オリーブ ¥500

TuNa & OLIVe

ツナ、ポテトスライス
オリーブ、グリーンカール

Supersize
sandwiches!

Photo by: yurina720

Insta-worthy! Veggie sandwiches bursting at the seams

Yoyogiuehara

✕ Potasta

How'd they pack so many veggies into the colorful Troublemaker Sandwich!? With crunchy lettuce and carrots sweet as honey, these seasonal vegetable sandwiches start from ¥500. There are no downsides to these delicious takeout sandwiches—they're a treat for your eyes and stomach, and they're good for you, too. On your next picnic, lay down your favorite blanket, make the greenery your backdrop, and strike a one-handed sandwich pose! A picnic selfie has never looked so good.

📍 3-16-11-102, Nishihara, Shibuya-ku

🚉 Yoyogiuehara Station

📞 03-5738-7545

🕐 7:30 am – 6:00 pm

🚫 Tuesdays

• Cross-section photos are a must.
• Try the dessert sandwiches, too.

Photo by: degu66/PIXTA

See the pink quilt of moss phlox in spring while it lasts!

Seibu Chichibu

📷 Hitsujiyama Park

Step into this spring wonderland as the sun's rays warm the air. Hitsujiyama Park (entry ticket ¥300) is a two-hour train ride from Ikebukuro, and waiting for you inside is a world of pink. Four hundred thousand plants of nine species of moss phlox are planted in a magnificent patchwork pattern across the gentle slopes. Walk between the stunning stretches of fuchsia, white, and purple, and look for the hidden heart-shaped patch.

📍 6360, Omiya, Chichibu-shi, Saitama

🚃 Seibu Chichibu Station and taxi

📞 0494-25-5209

🕐 24 hours (tickets required between 8:00 am – 5:00 pm)

🚫 –

- Try the famous Chichibu Potato Tempura with Miso.
- Pet some sheep at the petting zoo.

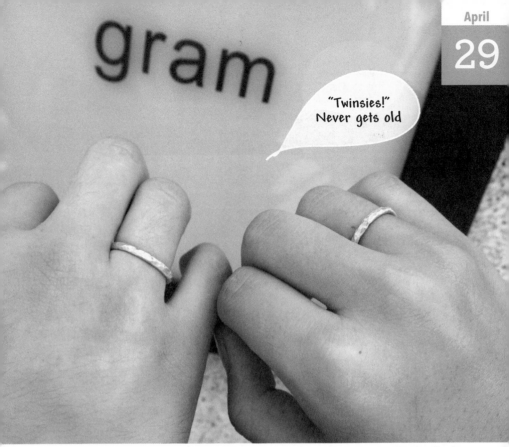

"Twinsies!" Never gets old

Photo by: Mihonchu

So many hearts touched! Personalize your own ring here

Kamakura

🎁 Kamakura Gram

All the fashion trendsetters are talking about this accessory shop. Invite your friend or partner to make one-of-a-kind jewelry with you! These made-to-order rings, anywhere from ¥990 to ¥5,990, are sized and crafted right in front of you. Delicate but loud; simple but unique, these statement pieces are proof that less is more. The modest price range lets you make more if you want to wear a stack of rings. Due to the shop's popularity, queue tickets are required, so get there early.

📍 1st Fl. 1-5-38, Yukinoshita, Kamakura-shi, Kanagawa

🚉 Kamakura Station

📞 0467-24-4232

🕐 11:00 am – 7:00 pm

🚫 –

- You can also make necklaces or earrings.
- Sit down for a *shirasu-don* (whitebait on rice) while you wait your turn, and get the most out of Kamakura.

April

30

A beachside film festival!

Starlit movies on the beach

Zushi

🚶 Zushi Beach Film Festival

Ever dream of watching a movie while sitting on a beach, with the sea breeze in your hair? The Zushi Beach Film Festival is here to make it come true. A screen is set up right on the sand, and both local and foreign films are projected every night. Before the movies start, browse the bazaar, chow down in the restaurants, and have fun in the workshops. When sunset dyes the sky orange, it's showtime. Enveloped by the sound of the tide under the skies, this will be an unforgettable evening.

📍 1-4, Shinjuku, Zushi-shi, Kanagawa

🚉 Zushi Station

📞 –

🕐 Check website

🚫 –

• Held annually during Golden Week (typically middle to end of May).
• Support local artists in the bazaar.

Wander through the wisteria

Ashikaga Flower Park

📷 Ashikaga Flower Park

In May, head to Ibaraki to bask in the transient beauty of the Wisteria Illumination. Chosen by CNN as one of the Top 10 Dream Destinations in the World, this sea of shimmering lavender almost looks computer generated. Even more charming is the reflection of the lights and flowers in the water below. Before you leave, be sure to try the fragrant Wisteria Soft Serve (¥400). The four-hour round trip from Tokyo is totally worth it.

📍 607, Hasamacho, Ashikaga-shi, Tochigi

🚆 Ashikaga Flower Park Station

📞 0284-91-4939

🕐 9:00 am – 6:00 pm
(subject to seasonal change)

🚫 Third Wednesday and Thursday of Feb., Dec. 31, irregular holidays (call first)

- Definitely take a group photo here.
- Love the smell of wisteria? Take it home in a bottle of fragrance.

That nostalgic feeling is part of the charm!

Tremble at the sight of Japan's oldest existing roller-coaster

Asakusa

🚶 Asakusa Hanayashiki

You'll want to include this retro amusement park in your Asakusa itinerary. Believe it or not, it opened in 1853. Scream your lungs out as you get launched into the air on Space Shot, take a ride on the melancholy-looking swans, and ride the oldest existing roller-coaster in Japan (built in 1953). The Hanayashiki original crepe, fruit and ice cream-filled Marion Hanayashiki is a must-try.

📍 2-28-1, Asaka, Taito-ku

🚃 Asakusa Station

📞 03-3842-8780

🕐 10:00 am – 6:00 pm
Note: Subject to seasonal, weather-related changes

🚫 None (excluding days for maintenance)

- Say hi to Brabo, Hanayashiki's personal matchmaking deity.
- The Japanese Festival Corner is full of retro fun.

A stress-free zone

Spend the eighty-eighth night in a quaint Japanese tea house

Jiyugaoka

✕ Kosoan Jiyugaoka

In Japan, it is said that tea made from leaves picked on the eighty-eighth day after Spring Equinox would bring good fortune to those who drank it. To get the most out of tea season, come to Kosoan in Jiyugaoka. Unwind in the relaxing atmosphere of a traditional Japanese home. The popular window seats offer a calming view of the garden. Savor the perfectly balanced *shiratama* (sweet dumpling) and red beans when you order the Kosoan-style Matcha Shiratama Zenzai. They also say drinking tea on the eighty-eighth night will bless you with longevity.

📍 1-24-23, Jiyugaoka, Meguro-ku

🚇 Jiyugaoka Station

📞 03-3718-4203

🕐 11:00 am – 6:30 pm

🚫 Wednesdays

- Take a look at the in-house gallery space.
- In summer, the seasonal matcha and lemon shaved ice is a must-try.

A classy edible souvenir will set you apart

The Japanese sweet shop to visit once a season

Ginza

Higashiya Ginza

Because oak trees do not shed leaves until they grow new ones, in Japan they are associated with family growth. Higashiya's Oak Leaf Mochi is made with delicious, sugar-free rice dough, and two types of filling are available: a sweet, elegant red bean paste and a deep, rich miso. Higashiya's seasonal desserts are released every solar term of the old lunisolar calendar (of which there are twenty-four), which means there's always something new and exciting to try. Check out the stylish in-store, modern Japanese Tea Salon.

📍 2nd Fl. POLA Ginza Bldg. 1-7-7, Ginza, Chuo-ku

🚇 Ginza Station

📞 03-3538-3230

🕐 11:00 am – 7:00 pm

🚫 –

- Oak leaf mochi (Japanese rice cake) available from early April to early May.
- Try their original tea blend in the tea salon.

These colorful carp are so photogenic!

Carp streamers swimming at the foot of Tokyo Tower

Akabanebashi

📷 333 Carp Streamers

In Japan, carp streamers are traditionally flown on May 5 for Children's Day. See the real thing for yourself at Tokyo Tower! Three hundred and thirty-three streamers of all sizes decorate the entry area to the tower each spring. Look up at them from the ground, and the vibrant carp will look like they're swimming in the sky with the tower as their backdrop. Hidden somewhere is a twenty-foot-long Mackerel Streamer, so keep your eyes peeled. At night, the hanging wires glow rainbow against the illuminated tower. You don't want to miss it.

📍 4-2-8, Shibakoen, Minato-ku

🚃 Akabanebashi Station

📞 03-3433-5111 (Tokyo Tower)

🕐 Please check the official website

🚫 –

• The streamers go up early April to early May.
• Check out the seasonal events at Tokyo Tower.

Indulgent snacks in a vintage shopping street

Tokyo's old-town snack, the croquette

Nippori

✕ Niku no Suzuki

Yanaka Ginza is an old-fashioned Japanese shopping strip that looks like a blast from the past. A hunt for street food should lead you to Niku no Suzuki's Croquette (¥110). These lovingly fried snacks are so good fresh. Careful, they're hot! If you're feeling indulgent, try the juicy Genki Menchikatsu (¥230), a fried ground-beef cutlet made with A5-grade beef. Did you know that May 6 is Croquette Day in Japan?

📍 3-15-5, Nishi-Nippori, Arakawa-ku

🚃 Nippori Station

📞 03-3821-4526

🕐 10:30 am – 6:00 pm

🚫 Mondays and Tuesdays

- Take the croquette with you as you explore Yanaka Ginza.
- Get the Torotoro BBQ Pork to go.

Hope the gods are listening!

Photogenic and spiritual

Todaimae

🚶 Nezu Shrine

The vermilion torii gates of Kyoto's Fushimi Inari are justly famous, but Tokyo boasts its own, equally stunning shrine. At Nezu Shrine, the trail leading up to Otome Inari is just as photoworthy. This stunning scenery is the result of years of prayers and offerings. It's only a small walk from Yanaka Ginza, so grab your camera, explore, and make a few wishes on the way.

📍 1-28-9, Nezu, Bunkyo-ku

🚃 Todaimae Station

📞 03-3822-0753

🕐 Shrine doors closing times:
Mar.–Sept.: 6:00 pm
Feb., Oct.: 5:30 pm
Nov.–Jan.: 5:00 pm

🚫 –

• Experience the Azalea Festival in April.
• In September, keep an eye out for the Three Edo Festivals.

Matchmaker, matchmaker, make me a match!

Swipe right on these love fortunes

Iidabashi

🚶 Tokyo Daijingu

Betting on luck to meet someone new? Visit the shrine rumored to find you a match if you offer prayer here! After your prayers, get your love fortune with *omikuji*. The love *omikuji* is crafted in pretty Japanese *washi* paper, and your fortune comes with a word of advice on your love life. There are several other types of *omikuji*, such as the Love Letter Omikuji—you'll have trouble picking just one!

📍 2-4-1, Fujimi, Chiyoda-ku

🚇 Iidabashi Station

📞 03-3262-3566

🕐 Open for prayers between 6:00 am – 9:00 pm

🚫 –

- Share the two-in-one Love Protection charm with your partner.
- For the wishes that really matter, write it down on an *ema* (wooden tablet for prayers and wishes).

Tasty and puffy!

The perfect snack for Ice Cream Day

Hiroo

✕ Melting in the Mouth

May 9 is Ice Cream Day in Japan! What better day to visit a shop with a unique version of soft serve? The adorably toy-like, puffy swirl is just the cutest thing. Simple but delicious, you can taste the effort they've put into ensuring the raw materials are fresh and organic. A little firmer than your regular soft serve, the rich flavor of the Original (¥480) melts in your mouth and leaves a refreshing aftertaste.

📍 1st Fl. 5-17-10, Hiroo, Shibuya-ku

🚆 Hiroo Station

📞 03-6459-3838

🕐 10:30 am – 8:30 pm

🚫 –

- Snap a pic of the Melted Ice Cream sculpture inside.
- Instagram followers can order from an exclusive menu.

This emerald green is SO Instagrammable

The emerald city of sandwiches

Shibuya

✗ Buy Me Stand

There are reasons why Buy Me Stand is rumored to be the best sandwich shop in Tokyo. Take a peek inside, and you'd almost believe you've been teleported across the Pacific Ocean into an American diner where everything is a stunning emerald green. Our recommendation is Blue Monday (¥1,200). You'll adore the unique, juicy flavor combination of orange and blue cheese. Oh, and coffee refills are free.

📍 1-31-19-302, Higashi, Shibuya-ku

🚇 Shibuya Station

📞 03-6450-6969

🕐 8:00 am – 9:00 pm

🚫 –

• Applecheeks is another popular favorite.
• Try both the sweet *and* spicy ginger ale.

Make out with the wall at the hippest café

Shibuya

✕ Flamingo

Fusion Street is full of character, but Flamingo's glowing crimson exterior sets itself far apart from the rest. The first thing you see when you step inside are flaming red, sexy lips. You might recognize some of the walls and decorations—this café is a popular location for promotional photoshoots and videos. Order a cream soda, and if you document your food, make sure you get the background in the picture. At night, the disco ball starts turning, and the café is transformed into a bar, so stay a little while longer.

📍 10-2, Udagawacho, Shibuya-ku

🚇 Shibuya Station

📞 03-6416-5513

🕐 11:30 am – 5:00 am
Sundays and last day of extended holiday: 11:30 am – 12:00 am

🚫 –

- Try the spicy Shibuya Keema Curry.
- The Peruvian ginseng-infused Shibuya Beer is worth a try!

A tour of Thai cuisine!

Photo by: Royal Thai Embassy, Tokyo

Experience Thailand without leaving Tokyo

Yoyogi-Koen

🚶 Thai Festival

Yoyogi Park is home to a series of cultural festivals year round. The popular Thai Festival, which delivers a Thai experience right here in central Tokyo, draws in three hundred thousand people every year. Watch traditional Thai dance performances while you have a Phuket beer and Pad Gaprao, and stuff your face with mango... you'll feel like you're in the street markets of Bangkok. Test your courage with durian from the fruit market, if you dare!

📍 2–1, Yoyogikamizonocho, Shibuya-ku

🚇 Yoyogi-Koen Station

📞 03-5789-2433 (Royal Thai Embassy, Tokyo)

🕐 10:00 am – 8:00 pm

🚫 –

- Get your fill of Tom Yum Kung and Pad Thai, too.
- Don't miss Muy Thai demonstrations and other performances.

Spirit yourself away!

May

13

Show Mom you care

Nakanojo

🏨 Sekizenkan Main Building

Take a trip to the oldest wooden hot spring *ryokan* (Japanese-style inn) in Japan. This is three hundred years of history condensed into one building, giving it an otherworldly vibe. It is said that the movie *Spirited Away* took inspiration from Sekizenkan. The red bridge, the building itself, even the tunnel leading up to the hotel grounds... it's as if *you've* been spirited away, and it's magical. The hot spring here is said to cure forty thousand illnesses, so take your time with a good, long soak.

📍 4236, Shima Ko, Nakanojomachi, Agatsumagun, Gunma

🚃 Nakanojo Station and bus

📞 0297-64-2101

🕐 Check-in: 2:00 pm – 6:00 pm
Check-out: 10:00 am

🚫 Rarely

- Don't forget to take a pic with Mom on the red bridge!
- Try the healthy *kaiseki* dinner.

It looks like a crimson rug!

Unwind in a painterly field of flowers

Nishitachikawa

🚶 Showa Kinen Park

Showa Kinen Park is about the size of forty baseball stadiums, and every spring it is home to the Flower Festival. In this metropolitan oasis, you can sit down for a relaxing picnic among brilliantly blooming tulips and poppies. Bicycles and boats are available for rent, and there is even a futsal court. This park is ideal for getting some exercise while surrounded by Mother Nature.

📍 3173, Midoricho, Tachikawa-shi

🚃 Nishi-Tachikawa Station

📞 042-528-1751

🕘 9:30 am – 5:00 pm (subject to seasonal or event changes)

🚫 New Year's holidays (12/31, 1/1), fourth Monday and following day of February

- There is also a pool and a barbecue area.
- Participate in the Tulip Bulb Dig in May.

Let's go to Okinawa this summer

Pretend you're in Okinawa!

Koenji

✕ Dachibin

A *dachibin* is an Okinawan ceramic flask. Set foot inside, and you're practically in Okinawa already. The friendly staff are dressed in traditional *eisa* dance garb, and are always ready to give a warm welcome. Celebrities from Okinawa are known to frequent Dachibin, contributing to its fame. Did you know Okinawa was returned to Japan on May 15, 1972? Come on in, everyone here has a story to tell.

📍 3-2-13, Koenjikita, Suginami-ku

🚃 Koenji Station

📞 03-3337-1352

🕐 5:00 pm – 5:00 am

🚫 –

- Pair *rafute* (Okinawa pork rib) and *champloo* (Okinawa stir fry) with some *awamori* (Okinawa rice liquor) for the full Okinawa experience.
- Everybody dances on folk music night.

Barhop till morning!

What'll you have tonight?

Ebisu

✗ Ebisu Yokocho

In elegant Ebisu, the red lanterns that line this street really stand out. If you want to drink on the streets of Tokyo, head over here. Ebisu Yokocho lights up at night into a chain of twenty colorful tiny bars, each only under 180 square feet. You have the ever-popular Meat Sushi, *oden*, barbecue skewers, seafood grill, Chinese street food, offal specialties, bistros, hostess bars, *teppanyaki*, mushroom cuisine and more... Don't know what you feel like tonight? You'll find something here. Any of these bars guarantee a good time.

📍	1-7-4, Ebisu, Shibuya-ku
🚇	Ebisu Station
📞	Depends on store
🕐	Depends on store
🚫	Depends on store

- You must try the raw meat sushi.
- Make it a challenge to dine at every bar.

Oh yeah,
that hits
the spot

The last dish of the night, the all-new ochazuke of Roppongi

Roppongi

✗ Creative Ochazuke Da Yo Ne

Spend May 17—Ochazuke (tea or broth over rice) Day in Japan—in Roppongi. The house broth here is simmered from a combination of konbu, flying fish, bonito, and more. End a fun night out with the heavenly Salmon and Roe Seafood Ochazuke, sure to soothe your belly after an evening of drinks. If you're hungry, we suggest the Scallop and Shrimp Burnt Butter Ochazuke. The smell of butter melting on seared seafood is enough to work up anyone's appetite.

📍 1st Fl. Kiyomizu Bldg. 4-12-4,
Roppongi, Minato-ku

🚇 Roppongi Station

📞 03-5770-5563

🕐 11:30 am – 12:00 am
Friday, Saturday, and days before
holidays: 11:30 am – 6:00 am
Sunday: 11:30 am – 12:00 am

🚫 –

- So good, you'll want to try every topping.
- Bar seats only, so you'll never feel lonely.

Rice makes the perfect stuffing here...

A challenger appears! The Ebisu BBQ turf war continues

Ebisu

✕ Ebisu Yoroniku

Ebisu Yoroniku is the new branch of the notoriously hard-to-book Yoroniku located in Minami-Aoyama. Relish top-grade beef such as Chateaubriand and *wagyu* with classic seasoning like salt and barbecue sauce, and try dipping them in raw egg yolk and their secret-recipe *ponzu* sauce. The rice balls, Silky Loin BBQ and Zabuton (a rare beef shoulder cut) Sukiyaki with Truffles will charm you into ordering seconds (and thirds), but make sure you leave some room! The popular fluffy shaved ice is waiting for you.

📍 8th Fl. 1-11-5, Ebisu, Shibuya-ku

🚇 Ebisu Station

📞 03-3440-4629

🕔 5:00 pm – 12:00 am

🚫 Mondays

- The Chateaubrian steak is way too enticing.
- The raw meat *nigiri* sushi is exquisite.

Hup! Hup!

Photo by: Asakusa Shrine

A seven hundred-year-old Japanese tradition

Asakusa

🚶 Asakusa Sanja Festival

If Asakusa is a main part of your itinerary, try to plan it around festival season. The *Sanja* Festival has been an annual tradition since the 1300s, and the stars of the show are the hundred *mikoshi*, or portable Shinto shrines. Carried on the backs of marching parishioners in traditional garb, the march is like a force of nature. In contrast, the Binzasara Dance, a performance with the traditional Japanese instrument *binzasara*, is slow and graceful. Pick up a candied apple and start by browsing the food stalls between Raimon and Bashamichi Street.

📍 2-3-1, Asakusa, Taito-ku

🚆 Asakusa Station

📞 03-3844-1575

🕐 Please check the official website

🚫 –

- The festival takes place across three days in mid-May.
- Only an Asakusa connoisseur can tell the difference between all the *mikoshi*.

Ooh, yeah... yoga in the sun

A free outdoor event: "lawn yoga"

Roppongi

🚶 Midpark Yoga

We're almost halfway through the year, and you deserve a break. Unwind your body and mind with some yoga. Midpark Yoga is a free event that takes place in the grassy outdoor space in Midtown. With spring in the air, about 350 people can come and relax for free. Don't worry if you're new to yoga— people of all ages and skill levels are welcome to participate. The instructors change daily, and it's a chance to learn new routines and new styles. Definitely give it a try!

📍 9-7-1, Akasaka, Minato-ku

🚆 Roppongi Station

📞 03-3475-3100

🕐 Please check the official website

🚫 –

• Night yoga while gazing up at Tokyo Tower sounds great, too.
• Energize your body with morning yoga.

A different take on the *oyakodon*

A literary master's favorite old-establishment oyakodon

Shimbashi

✗ Suegen

In the mood for a protein-packed power lunch? Come to Suegen. This restaurant has been around since 1909, and their incredible *oyakodon* (chicken and egg on rice), the Kama Set, is made with ground chicken instead of cubed chicken thigh. The chicken soup is also not to be underestimated. In fact, Japanese literary master Yukio Mishima chose Suegen as the place for his last meal. Don't miss the chance to try the chicken broth hot pot course, *Wa*.

📍 2-15-7, Shimbashi, Minato-ku

🚃 Shimbashi Station

📞 03-3591-6214

🕐 11:30 am – 1:30 pm
5:30 pm – 10:00 pm

🚫 Saturday (irregular),
Sunday, holidays

- Deep-fried chicken meals are also available.
- The *Wa* dinner course starts from ¥8,000.

Happiness is fluffy, rich, and jiggly

Photo by: komaya

The omelet of a long-established café

Higashi-Ginza

✗ Café You

Apparently May 22 is Egg Cuisine Day. Make it an occasion by going to Café You for their Omelet Rice (lunch set approx. ¥1,100). Not only will you want to take a video of this perfect egg dome jiggling, but also document the thick, rich, scrambled egg oozing out as you take a spoon to it. Top it off with some ketchup, and see for yourself how the acidity highlights the delicious taste in your mouth. Look for the green neon sign to find the entrance.

📍 1st, 2nd Fl. 4-13-17, Ginza, Chuo-ku

🚃 Higashi-Ginza Station

📞 03-6226-0482

🕐 11:00 am – 8:00 pm

🚫 New Year's holidays

- No, really. Take the jiggly video.
- Try the Egg Sandwich, too.

Take time to smell the roses

Note: Flower growth depends on season. Photo taken Mid- to late May.

The botanical garden to visit during rose season

Hiranumabashi

🚶 Yokohama English Garden

May is rose season, so come to Yokohama to get an eyeful. Blooming in Yokohama English Garden are over 1,800 species of roses in red, pink, yellow, and more. They converge at the main attraction, the 164-foot-long Rose Tunnel. Dress up in something floral! After making some memories, sit down for a Rose Lemonade at the café. Don't forget to pick up some rose tea at the gift store. Today, life *is* a bed of roses.

📍 6-1, Nishi-Hiranumacho, Nishi-ku, Yokohama, Kanagawa

🚃 Hiranumabashi Station

📞 045-326-3670

🕐 10:00 am – 6:00 pm

🚫 New Year's holidays

- If you're lucky, you might see some hydrangeas.
- The garden also offers Rose Workshops. (Not available in May.)

May

24

A detour... to "Europe"?

Photo by: Takanawa Princess Garten

A romantic date on cobblestone roads

Shinagawa

🚶 Takanawa Princess Garten

A six-minute walk through the quiet residential area of Shinagawa will take you to a quaint space filled with sunbeams. This replica of the German streets of Rothenburg is authentic and impressive. Almost all of the materials used in the construction, including the cobblestones, were imported from Germany. Spend a day lounging on the outdoor benches with your loved ones, or enjoy a concert in one of their performance halls. For a romantic date experience, end the night at one of the French restaurants on garden grounds.

📍 4-24-40, Takanawa, Minato-ku

🚇 Shinagawa Station

📞 03-3443-1521

🕐 Depends on facility

🚫 Depends on facility

- Bask in the light spilling through the leaves.
- The nighttime illuminations are just as romantic.

Today, we live the high life

For some high-end shopping, come to Ginza

Ginza

✣ Tokyu Plaza Ginza

This contemporary building is a symbol of ever-changing, rapidly evolving Ginza. Check for the newest trends in the display windows, then head to the restaurant floors. Take a break at Sukiyabashi-Sabo on the sixth floor, and take in the view of the city through the Japanese glasswork-style windows. Before you leave, pick up a snack for later at Granny Smith Apple Pie & Coffee.

📍	5-2-1, Ginza, Chuo-ku
🚇	Ginza Station
📞	03-3571-0109
🕐	Depends on store
🚫	Irregular days, New Year's holidays

- There are over 120 stores to shop at.
- Have lunch at Ramen Keisuke.

The café you could visit just for the tables

Omotesando

✗ Nicolai Bergmann Nomu

In the alleyways of Omotesando is an influencer's dream. It's Danish flower artist Nicolai Bergmann's flower shop-cum-café, and it's too stylish for words. Polish off a healthy Danish open sandwich, then order a fruit tart (¥648) and smoothie. Just remember to take a photo of them with the seasonal flower arrangement table before you dig in!

📍 5-7-2, Minami-Aoyama, Minato-ku

🚇 Omotesando Station

📞 03-5464-0824

🕐 10:00 am – 8:00 pm

🚫 Irregular

- The Flower Boxes make a fantastic gift.
- Flower workshops are held on the second floor.

An essential part of every trip to Ginza

The face of Ginza you'll want to see

Ginza

🎁 Ginza Six

Ginza Six is the largest commercial complex in Ginza. Its modern atrium is home to 241 stores and leaves quite an impression. Take a look at the food section of the store list, and you'll see that the dessert selection is almost overwhelming... There are too many choices and too little time! The *matcha* parfait at Nakamura Tochiki, the Smoothie Bonbon from Elle Café, pies from American favorite The Pie Hole Los Angeles... There's no way you'll go home empty-handed—or empty-bellied!

📍 6-10-1, Ginza, Chuo-ku

🚇 Ginza Station

📞 03-6891-3390

🕐 Shops: 10:30 am – 8:30 pm
Restaurants: 11:00 am – 11:30 pm

🚫 Irregular

- You could spend all day in Ginza Tsutaya Books.
- The view from the rooftop garden, almost one acre in size, is splendid.

A little bit of luxury is necessary once in a while

Seasonal dessert to try at Ginza Six

Ginza

✗ Café Dior by Pierre Hermé

Treat yourself to some high-end teatime. This is the first collaborative café of its kind in Japan. The desserts here are made from premium local ingredients and served on beautiful tableware from Christian Dior's collections. Excitingly, the menu changes with the seasons. They say renowned French pastry chef Pierre Hermé himself takes over the kitchen whenever he's in Japan, creating new, unique desserts for people to enjoy. Try one yourself today.

📍 4th Fl. 6-10-1, Ginza, Chuo-ku

🚉 Ginza Station

📞 03-3569-1085

🕐 10:30 am – 8:30 pm

🚫 Irregular

- Pay attention to the gorgeous Christian Dior tableware.
- Mellow out with the fragrant tea selection.

No cilantro for the rest of the month, please...

Work up a sweat with Cilantro Hot Pot

Nakano

✗ Thai Food-stall Restaurant 999

When summer rolls around, do you find yourself reaching for something spicy? May 29 is Southeast Asia Appreciation Day, and if you find yourself craving Thai food, head over to 999 (pronounced "kaokaokao"). See how much cilantro you can take in one sitting with their famous Cilantro Hot Pot. Challengers can even order extra. More good news for herb-lovers: on the eighth, ninth, and twentieth of every month, pay just ¥99 for all-you-can-eat cilantro.

📍 1st Fl. 5-53-10, Nakano, Nakano-ku

🚌 Nakano Station

📞 03-3386-0383

🕐 11:30 am – 2:00 pm
5:30 am – 1:00 am

🚫 Mondays (open if holiday)

• The all-you-can-eat special is limited to nine tables a day on weekdays.
• Wrap up the night with Hainanese Chicken Rice.

Who doesn't love tacos?

Photo by: Hacienda del cielo

The Mexican restaurant with a view of Daikanyama

Daikanyama

✗ Hacienda del Cielo

One of the best places to eat lunch and dinner in one of the trendiest areas of Tokyo, Daikanyama, is Hacienda del Cielo, or Estate in the Sky. It lives up to its name—the terrace seats give you a sweeping view of the city while you enjoy Mexican cuisine like tacos or tortillas. The holiday lunch comes with appetizer and dessert for just ¥1,700, and the dinner comes with a view of Tokyo Tower all lit up. *Me gusta!*

📍 9th Fl. 10-1, Sarugakucho, Shibuya-ku

🚃 Daikanyama Station

📞 03-5457-1521

🕐 11:30 am – 1:30 am
Fridays, days before holidays:
11:00 am – 3:30 am
Saturdays: 11:00 am – 3:30 am

🚫 Irregular

- If you're on a date, ask for the two-seater sofa seats.
- Try the five-tequila taster set.

Wonderful in every season

The hot spring with an ever-changing view of the seasons

Karuizawa

🚶 Hoshino Resorts Tombo-no-yu

Karuizawa's Hoshino hot spring has over one hundred years of history to its name. It was opened to the public in 1915, and is also known for having accommodated famous guests like Japanese poets Hakushu Kitahara and Yosano Akiko. The open windows give visitors a breathtaking view of the lush greenery of summer, the soft snow of winter, and the ever-shifting seasons in between. The hot spring water bubbling straight from the source is said to be good for your skin. Enjoy the remarkable view, celebrated architecture, and famous hot springs.

📍 Hoshino, Karuizawacho, Nagano

🚌 Karuizawa Station and bus

📞 0267-44-3580

🕐 10:00 am – 11:00 pm
Note: Subject to seasonal change

🚫 –

• If you get peckish, Harunire Terrace restaurant is right next door.
• There's nothing like a hot spring experience in snowy winter.

Photo by: Edo-Tokyo Open Air Architecture Museum

Bring a few rolls of film or extra storage cards, you'll need them!

Musashi-Koganei

🚶 Edo-Tokyo Open Air Architecture Museum

June 1 is Photograph Day, and there's no shortage of things and places to capture at this outdoor museum. This museum relocates and restores historically important post-Edo period architecture (entry ticket is approx. ¥400). Here, you can go back in time to capture images of Japanese architecture anywhere from the mid-1800s to the 1980s. Bring an instant or film camera for retro-feel results.

📍 3-7-1, Sakuracho, Koganei-shi

🚉 Musashi-Koganei Station and bus

📞 042-388-3300

🕐 9:30 am – 5:30 pm
Note: Subject to seasonal change

🚫 Mondays (open if holiday),
New Year's holidays

- Take a new profile pic here.
- Try the traditional Musashino Dip Udon Noodles.

Photo by: pullwell/PIXTA

The park with a sea breeze

Daiba

🚶 Shiokaze Park

Get your fill of outdoor life before the rainy season sets in. If you're in the mood for fresh air and plants, you'll want to head to this park with tropical vibes. Following a promenade lined with street lamps and palm trees, you'll come to a beautiful fountain plaza facing Tokyo Bay. The coast deck gives you a clear view of the ocean, and a stroll never felt so liberating. There's plenty of grass to relax on, and even a barbecue area, so call up your friends and family and get ready for a good time.

📍 Higashiyashio, Shinagawa-ku

🚉 Daiba Station

📞 03-5500-2455

🕐 24 hours

🚫 –

- The view of the sun setting into Tokyo Bay is worth waiting for.
- The night view of Rainbow Bridge is spectacular.

Take the wheel as the first mate!

Roleplay on the first Japanese Antarctic observation vessel

Tokyo International Cruise Terminal

🚶 Museum of Maritime Science

True to its name, this ship-shaped museum is a common field-trip destination. The main attraction, *Soya*, Japan's first Antarctic observation vessel, was restored and reopened to the public in 2017. See for yourself what the navigation room, engine room, or mess deck were like when the ship was in operation. The bright orange paint, meant to help the ship stand out at sea, looks gallant even at port.

📍 3-1, Higashiyashio, Shinagawa-ku

🚇 Tokyo International Cruise Terminal Station

📞 03-5500-1111

🕐 10:00 am – 5:00 pm

🚫 Mondays (open if holiday), New Year's holidays

- Commemorate your trip with a photo in front of all 275 feet of *Soya*'s glory.
- Experience the wintering crew's life on the hands-on tour.

Photo by: deco no Kaze/PIXTA

From the final scene of Your Name

Yotsuya-sanchome

🚶 # Suga Shrine

Does this photo look familiar? The last scene from animated feature hit *Your Name* takes place on the steps leading up to Suga Shrine. Be amazed at how perfectly the film captured this exact location. Because of its elevated position, the air of Suga Shrine is fresh and clean. Make sure to leave your prayers and offerings before you go. The shrine's annual festival activities take place in June, so plan your visit accordingly.

📍 5, Sugacho, Shinjuku-ku

🚃 Yotsuya-sanchome Station

📞 03-3351-7023

🕐 Open for prayers 9:00 am – 5:00 pm

🚫 –

- Re-enact the scene from the movie.
- Other locations around the shrine are also featured in the film.

It's the café from *Your Name!*

Teatime in Tokyo? Choose an art museum

Nogizaka

🚶 The National Art Center, Tokyo

Head to an art museum just for its trendy café? Why not? The café practically floats on the second floor of the atrium, surrounded by trees and the sun filtering through the gentle curve of the glass walls. An elegant time awaits you here, along with exhibitions featuring both classic and contemporary art. Some people may remember seeing the café in the famous animated feature film *Your Name*—are you one of them?

📍 7-22-2, Roppongi, Minato-ku

🚇 Nogizaka Station

📞 03-5777-8600 (call center)

🕐 10:00 am – 6:00 pm
Open until 8:00 pm on Fridays and Saturdays during exhibitions.

🚫 Tuesdays (open if holiday, closed following business day)

- The exhibition tie-in menus change regularly.
- Day-care service available (reservation required).

Rich flavors and natural sweetness

Savor delicious treats from a traditional Japanese confectionary

Azabu-Juban

✗ Shiroikuro

A stone's throw from the Azabu-Juban Station, Shiroikuro is famous for its traditional and innovative Japanese sweets, cakes, and ice creams, specially made with black soybeans. The Kyoto-style *kuromame shio daifuku*—salted mochi dumplings filled with black bean paste—is their most popular dessert, but their specialty roll cakes are a must-try. Get there early and satisfy your sweet cravings!

📍 2-8-1, Azabu-Juban, Minato-ku

🚋 Azabu-Juban Station

📞 03-3454-7225

🕐 10:00 am – 6:00 pm

🚫 Irregular, holidays

- Limited number of desserts per day.
- Menu is seasonal.

That butter smells SO good

Photo by: aloha6misato

Breakfast at a café to start off the day

Omotesando

✗ Crisscross

Come to this café in the alleyways of Minami-Aoyama for a taste of heaven in the form of the Classic Buttermilk Pancake (¥900). There's no feeling of happiness like maple syrup-drenched pancake dissolving in your mouth, especially eaten sitting in an open terrace sheltered by camphor trees. The café is open all day, but it's at its best in the morning. Start your day with this, and nothing will get you down.

📍 5-7-28, Minami-Aoyama, Minato-ku

🚊 Omotesando Station

📞 03-6434-1266

🕐 8:00 am – 9:00 pm

🚫 –

• Pancakes are also available during lunch and dinner time.
• At night, wrap up your day with a craft beer or two.

Ask for extra sauce on your rice!

Pad Gaprao for just ¥68?!

Shibuya

✗ Gapao Shokudo

Want cheap Pad Gaprao? Come to Gapao Shokudo on June 8. This restaurant has declared that date (the day they opened) Gaprao Day for good reason: their mission is to popularize Pad Gaprao in Japan. Their signature Pad Gaprao is ¥1,058 on any other day, but today it is an inconceivable, incredible, insane ¥68! The taste of Thai basil (Gaprao) in combination with other Thai spices is to die for. They say spicy food can give your metabolism a boost, so eat up!

📍 1st Fl. 2-8-10, Shibuya, Shibuya-ku

🚆 Shibuya Station

📞 03-3797-9937

🕐 11:30 am – 2:00 pm
6:00 pm – 11:30 pm
Note: Dinners start at 5:00 on weekends and holidays

🚫 New Year's holidays

- Try their Tom Yum Kung and Thai Curry, too.
- Give your body what it needs with Thai spices and herbs.

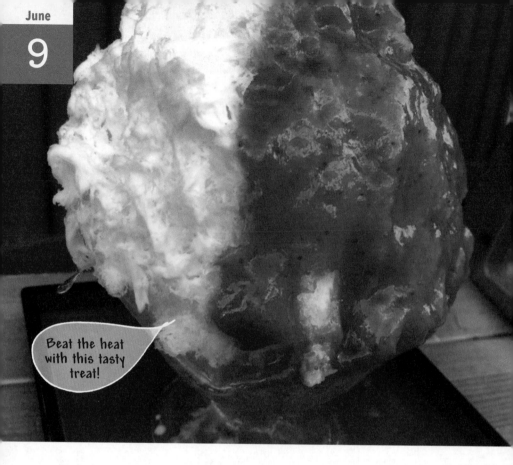

Beat the heat with this tasty treat!

Cool down with delicious traditional Japanese shaved ice

Nippori

✗ Himitsudo

A charming eatery located in Yanaka Ginza, Himitsudo specializes in traditional *kakigori*, shaved ice desserts, that come in a variety of delicious flavors. The ice is shaved using a hand-operated machine and fruit juices are used instead. Additionally, there are over 130 seasonal homemade syrups! Try a classic strawberry shaved ice or choose a more unique flavor, such as the *Uguisu-Zakura* (green tea and cherry blossom). Whatever you pick, you can't go wrong!

📍	3-11-18, Yanaka, Taito-ku
🚇	Nippori Station
📞	03-3824-4132
🕐	About 10:00 am – 5:00 pm Open from 8:00 am in summer, 9:00 am on weekends
🚫	Closed on Mondays Closed on Tuesdays Oct. – June

- Tickets for entry may be allocated on busy days.
- Visit their website and Twitter to confirm shop timings and holidays.

Get smashed on all-you-can-drink plum wine

Shibuya

Shugar Market Shibuya

June 10 is Plum Day. There's no better excuse to spend a night indulging on plum wine, right? Here, the selection of over one hundred types of plum wine and fruit liquors is unlimited. The Plum and Fruit Wine All-You-Can-Taste Course has, if you can believe it, no time limit. Thick plum wine, sour plum wine, strawberry plum wine... you won't be able to get enough! Bring your own food, and if you run out, you are free to leave and pick up more. Is this heaven?

- 3rd Fl. 2-9-2, Dogenzaka, Shibuya-ku
- Shibuya Station
- 03-6455-1997
- 5:00 pm - 11:00 pm
  Weekends: 12:00 pm - 4:00 pm
  5:00 pm - 11:00 pm
- –

- You don't see pumpkin and chestnut liquor every day.
- Bring your favorite snacks to pair with the plum wine.

Photo by: Penguin Bar Ikebukuro

Grab a drink in Tokyo... with penguins

Ikebukuro

✗ Penguin Bar Ikebukuro

There are plenty of fun, themed bars in Tokyo that make you laugh or scratch your head, and this is one of them. Most of us don't get a chance to see penguins outside of aquariums or zoos, but here, you can drink with them. If you're lucky, you might even get a chance to feed them. Even the food comes with adorable penguin-motif decorations.

📍 1st Fl. 2-38-2, Ikebukuro, Toshima-ku

🚊 Ikebukuro Station

📞 03-5927-1310

🕐 6:00 pm – 4:00 am
Sundays and last day of extended holidays: 6:00 pm – 1:00 am

🚫 –

• Feeding time is usually around 7:00 pm – 8:00 pm.
• The drink menu is extensive.

The most authentic southern Indian curry!

June 12 is the Day of Love and Revolution and Indian Curry

Nakameguro

✗ Sri Balaj

It may sound unbelievable, but in Japan, this is an actual registered day of the year. If you're curious about its origins, look up the incredible story of Rash Behari Bose and his wife, Toshiko Bose. And have you ever seen an Indian restaurant this cute? It's the perfect place to celebrate the day. The chairs, window frames, and even the washrooms are pink. Their all-you-can-eat weekday lunches are just ¥1,000. Southern Indian curries use less oil and spices and are mild and mellow. The rice batter "dosa" and Indian-style pizzas are recommended.

📍 2-7-14, Nakameguro, Meguro-ku

🚉 Nakameguro Station

📞 03-5724-8995

🕐 11:00 am – 2:30 pm
5:00 pm – 10:30 pm

🚫 –

• Take pictures of the incredible interior.
• Definitely order the amazing cheese naan.

Stand out in
the rain with a
unique umbrella

Four floors of just umbrellas in this specialty shop

Jiyugaoka

🎁 Waterfront

You'll want an umbrella handy for Japan's rainy season, so why not make it one you love? This is one of the largest umbrella specialty stores in the world. Functionality, design, lightness... whatever your needs are, there's something for you here. They even have prefecture-themed umbrellas! With over ten thousand umbrellas to choose from, the variety is endless. Find the umbrella that sets you apart on a dreary day. The wide selection for people of all ages and sizes makes this a perfect place to find a unique gift.

📍 1-9-1, Jiyugaoka, Meguro-ku

🚃 Jiyugaoka Station

📞 03-6421-2108

🕙 11:00 am – 8:00 pm

🚫 Irregular

- The umbrellas lined up like books on shelves are photo-worthy.
- The functionality test corner is fun.

Hydrangea season is upon us!

Photo by: @c.tak_tr(takumichiyo)

A stunning sight reserved for the rainy season

Hakusan

🚶 Bunkyo Hydrangea Festival

The highlight of the walk between Hakusan Shrine and Hakusan Park are the colorful hydrangeas growing along the path in vibrant pink, blue, and purples. There are over twenty species and three thousand individual plants. On the weekends, there's an abundance of booths you'll find nowhere else, like potted hydrangea vendors or offering boxes for toothbrushes (the Hakusan Shrine is home to the god of toothache cures!). Don't hate on the rainy season—make the most of it while it lasts.

📍 5-31-26, Hakusan, Bunkyo-ku

🚉 Hakusan Station

📞 03-3811-6568

🕘 9:00 am – 5:00 pm

🚫 –

• The festival usually takes place over nine days in the first half of June.
• There are four other flower festivals in Bunkyo-ku.

Find the flower of your dreams in the most stylish of places

Omotesando

🎁 Country Harvest

After a day of appreciating flowers from afar, it's time to look for some to take home with you. The fresh green exterior of this flower shop is both cute and cool, and the shop's theme is, as its name suggests, a country harvest. With flower arrangements, extravagance is often a given, but Country Harvest specializes in subtlety. Ask the shop staff for recommendations. They're sure to suggest beautiful blue flowers such as hydrangea and delphinium to light up your life.

📍 3-13-13, Minami-Aoyama, Minato-ku

🚃 Omotesando Station

📞 03-5410-1481

🕐 10:00 am – 8:00 pm
Sundays and holidays:
10:00 am – 6:00 pm

🚫 New Year's holidays

- Order an original bouquet here.
- Brush up on your design sense with their workshops.

True luxury is a high-class Japanese dessert

Wagashi day demands the chewy warabimochi

Hongo-sanchome

✕ Kurogi

On a hot, humid day, cool down with some chilled wagashi, or Japanese sweets. Their *Warabimochi*, or bracken starch jelly-cake, comes in a bowl shaped like Kurogi's logo. One half holds the mochi soaking in ice water, and in the other half are *kinako* (roasted sweet soy powder) and green *kinako* for dipping. The bracken starch used to make their *warabimochi* can only be harvested from five percent of the plant, and the result is a beautiful, bouncy jelly. By the way, June 16 is Wagashi Day.

📍 Daiwa Ubiquitous Research Building 1st Fl. 7-3-1, Hongo, Bunkyo-ku

🚃 Hongo-sanchome Station

📞 03-5802-5577

🕐 9:00 am – 6:00 pm

🚫 –

- Have a few cups of Zarutahiko Coffee.
- Get there at 9:00 am for a morning shaved ice.

Dads deserve a bit more love!

For Father's Day, give dad a rooftop open-air hot spring experience

Kinugawa Onsen

🏨 Kinugawa Hot Springs Asaya Hotel

For Father's Day, take Dad on a hot spring retreat. Kinugawa Hot Springs is a hot spring village just two hours from Asakusa on the Tobu Railway. The view of the river valley from Kurogane Bridge is extraordinary. Soak in the highest open-air hot spring of Kinugawa Hot Springs at Asaya Hotel, which has 130 years of history under its belt. The view of the starry skies and the cityscape is an opulent treat.

📍 813, Kinugawaonsentaki, Nikko-shi, Tochigi

🚉 Kinugawa Onsen Station and bus

📞 0288-77-1111

🕐 Check-in 3:00 pm
Check-out 10:00 am

🚫 –

- The buffet dinner serves over one hundred dishes!
- Try ziplining at Kinu River (*Kinu-gawa*).

Enjoy Japanese soul food

June

18

Eat delicious Japanese rice balls made with a variety of fillings

Nakameguro

✕ Onigily Cafe

Start your day at the Onigily Café. Situated in fashionable Nakameguro, this popular neighborhood hangout is the place to go to for delicious Onigiri, traditional Japanese rice balls, served with an assortment of tasty fillings. What's more, for affordable prices, you can enjoy their breakfast set which comes with your choice of two onigiri, pickled cucumbers, miso soup, and a beverage. If you're in a rush, just ask their friendly staff to pack a takeout set and they will be more than happy to!

📍 3-1-4, Nakameguro, Meguro-ku

🚇 Nakameguro Station

📞 03-5708-5342

🕐 8:00 am – 4:00 pm

🚫 –

• There are over twenty onigiri to choose from.

Coffee break, anyone?

Stroll in the park between spring showers, coffee in hand

Inokashira Park

✗ Blue Sky Coffee

When the rainy season finally hits pause, it's time to get some sun. And that means a trip to Inokashira Park is in order. Get coffee to go from a store with a perfect name for the occasion. Fitting for Inokashira Park, home to both real swans and swan boats, each cup is printed with a swan silhouette so cute, you can't help but take a picture. If you like the coffee, pick up some of their home-roasted beans to enjoy at home.

📍 Inside Inokashira Park, 4-1-1, Inokashira, Mitaka-shi

🚃 Inokashira Park Station

📞 —

🕐 10:00 am – 6:00 pm

🚫 Sundays, and in rainy weather

- You may recognize the shop from its TV appearances.
- Hot wines, ales, and beer are available, too.

Climb this spiral staircase!

The museum that combines art and nature

Chokoku-no-Mori

🚶 The Hakone Open-Air Museum

While Hakone is famous for its hot springs, another way to enjoy the town is to tour its museums. The Hakone Open-Air Museum is the first outdoor museum of Japan, in which you can see around 120 pieces of art in its seventeen-acre garden. A giant face in a pool of water, a castle of bubbles, oversized sunny-side-up eggs...you could spend all day around these sculptures. The museum's centerpiece is the showstopping stained glass tower, Symphonic Sculpture.

📍 1121, Ninoshita, Hakonemachi, Ashigarashimogun, Kanagawa

🚃 Chokoku-no-Mori Station

📞 0460-82-1161

🕘 9:00 am – 5:00 pm

🚫 –

- The Picasso Collection is a must-see.
- Don't forget to take a break at the outdoor foot bath.

Moss is so pretty!

Enjoy the rainy season in a moist moss garden

Gora

🚶 Hakone Museum of Art's Moss Garden

Moss soaks up every drop of rain in June, becoming more vibrant as it does so. The garden at Hakone Museum of Art is called Shinsenkyou ("the home of gods"). Around 130 species of moss and two hundred Japanese maple trees make up the Moss Garden. After a stroll around, stop by the tea house, Shinwatei, for seasonal desserts, sustainably farmed *matcha*, and another good look at the greenery outside.

📍 1300 Gora, Hakonemachi, Ashigarashimogun, Kanagawa

🚆 Gora Station and cablecar

📞 0460-82-2623

🕐 9:30 am – 4:30 pm (subject to seasonal change)

🚫 Thursday (open if holiday or in November), New Year's Holidays

- Be sure to check out the museum and its collections.
- You can purchase tea sets at the museum shop.

The adrenaline rush of making it to the top!

If it's sunny, try outdoor rock climbing

Ochanomizu

🚶 B-Pump Tokyo

Stay indoors on rainy days, or head outside when it clears up at this all-weather rock-climbing gym. Never tried it before? Why not make today the day here at B-Pump? All you have to do is dress comfortably, as shoe and chalk rentals are available. Staff members offer free lessons, no reservations needed. Look no further to shake off that rainy season cabin fever.

📍 1-1-8, Yushima, Bunkyo-ku

🚉 Ochanomizu Station

📞 03-6206-9189

🕐 12:00 pm – 11:00 pm
Saturdays and holidays:
11:00 am – 10:00 pm
Sundays: 10:00 am – 9:00 pm

🚫 –

- Beginner-friendly workshops available (¥4,320).
- Find a souvenir at the B-Pump shop.

June
23

Trampoline workout today!

Have fun and get a good workout

Itabashikuyakushomae

🚶 Trampoline Park Trampoland

Still June, still raining. If you're feeling cramped and need to let off some steam, head to a trampoline park for some fun exercise (approx. ¥1,620/hr.). While you bounce around, high on adrenaline, you'll get a strenuous full-body workout. Just jumping around can, in fact, work you harder than a light jog, so it's great exercise and fun at the same time!

📍 2-46-3, Itabashi, Itabashi-ku

🚃 Itabashikuyakushomae Station

📞 03-6322-6966

🕐 1:00 pm – 10:00 pm
Weekends and holidays:
10:00 am – 8:00 pm (open
only to children until noon)

🚫 Mondays (open on holiday
Mondays and closed next
business day)

• Mid-air photo opportunities aplenty!
• The newest trampolines are imported straight from the USA.

You're in luck if blue's your favorite color!

Photo by: genki / PIXTA

A blue approach for the rainy season

Kita-Kamakura

📷 Meigetsu-in Temple

The most renowned spot in the Kanto area for hydrangea viewing. With 2,500 hydrangea plants blooming along the path leading up to the temple, it's no wonder Meigetsu-in Temple is also known as the "hydrangea temple." Along the rickety steps, lush greenery is polka dotted in "Meigetsuin blue," and you'll find yourself climbing into a visual fantasy. The scenery draws a crowd every year, so you'll want to get there early. The massive circular Window of Enlightenment in the main temple is another awe-inspiring sight you won't want to miss.

📍 189, Yamanouchi, Kamakura-shi, Kanagawa

🚉 Kita-Kamakura Station

📞 0467-24-3437

🕘 9:00 am – 4:00 pm (8:30 – 5:00 pm in June)

🚫 –

- Look for that super-rare heart-shaped hydrangea.
- The Window of Enlightenment is splendid in autumn.

June

25

Prepare to gasp at this view!

Photo by: Tsunetoshi Sato

A sea of clouds, just ninety minutes out of Tokyo

Chichibu/Minano

📷 Minoyama Park

This seasonal miracle is worth the trip. Mount Mino (Minoyama) is 1,906 feet tall, and covered in hydrangea plants that go into full bloom at the end of June each year. Under the right conditions, you might be lucky enough to see a field of hydrangea floating in a sea of clouds. If, after a storm, the sun graces a windless morning, this miraculous visual feast might appear for early risers. Rub those sleepy eyes—this is the view of a lifetime.

📍 2372, Kuroya, Chichibu-shi, Saitama

🚃 Minano Station and Taxi

📞 0494-23-1511 (Chichibu City Environment Management Office)

🕐 24 hours

🚫 —

- The night view made it into the Top 100 Night Views of Japan list!
- Flower season is perfect for hiking.

Experience a fun-filled day in Yokohama's quirky new entertainment complex!

Yokohama

🚶 ASOBUILD

Spend the day at ASOBUILD, Japan's new, first-of-its-kind entertainment complex, and enjoy many unique and exciting experiences. Once the annex of the Yokohama Central Post Office, today this four-story building—each floor designed with a different theme—boasts top-notch restaurants, the latest technology, innovative escape games and exhibition events, a Kids Park, multi-sports courts, and more.

📍	2-14-9 Takashima, Nishi-ku, Yokohama-shi, Kanagawa
🚃	Yokohama Station
📞	–
🕐	10:00 am – 10:00 pm (Depending on each floor)
🚫	Irregular holidays

- Easy access to the Yokohama Station
- Fun activities for all ages!

Immerse yourself in art

teamLab, *The Infinite Crystal Universe*, 2018, Interactive Installation of Light Sculpture, LED, Endless, Sound: teamLab © teamLab

Experience a one-of-a-kind, "body immersive" digital-art exhibition

Shin-Toyosu

📷 teamLab Planets TOKYO

teamLab Planets is a museum unlike any other. Filled with interactive digital artworks created by top-notch specialists, visitors can literally immerse themselves in the art. Experience a 360-degree view of flowers blooming and changing over a season in *Floating in the Falling Universe of Flowers* or walk barefoot through water and light in *Drawing on the Water Surface Created by the Dance of Koi and People - Infinity*. The different exhibitions will be sure to take your breath away.

📍 Toyosu 6-1-16, Koto-ku

🚊 Shin-Toyosu Station

📞 –

🕐 Mondays – Thursdays:
10:00 am – 7:00 pm
Fridays: 10:00 am – 9:00 pm
Saturdays, days before holidays:
9:00 am – 9:00 pm
Sundays and holidays:
9:00 am – 7:00 pm

🚫 –

- The exhibition will conclude in Fall 2020.
- No shoes or socks allowed inside.

Dream about the perfect staycation here

Hang out in a hammock

Shimokitazawa

✗ Café Stay Happy

With the rainy season coming to an end, it's time to plan your summer vacation in a lovely café like Café Stay Happy. At the center of this warm, natural space are hammock seats hanging boldly from wooden beams. Lie down for a swing and fantasize about future travel plans. The owner has been all over the world, and may be able to give you some tips. At night, the café hosts workshops and lectures on traveling and backpacking. Give them a go.

📍 2nd Fl. 2-29-14, Daizawa, Setagaya-ku

🚉 Shimokitazawa Station

📞 03-3410-5959

🕐 1:00 pm – 11:00 pm
Sundays: 1:00 pm – 10:00 pm

🚫 Tuesdays, second Wedesday of every month

• Vegetables used in Stay Happy's dishes come directly from organic farms in Chiba.
• In winter, *kotatsu* seats (at blanketed, heated low tables) are available.

Konnichiwa!

Leading Tokyo's guesthouse culture

Kuramae

🏨 Nui. Hostel & Bar Lounge

This super on-trend guest house was renovated from an old toy factory warehouse. Pictured above is the bar lounge on the first floor, and it's open to everyone. A look through the glass facade at travelers mingling entices you to join them. The location is ideal for sight-seeing in Asakusa or old-town Tokyo. Darn, should have brushed up on a few more languages before coming!

📍	2-14-13, Kuramae, Taito-ku
🚃	Kuramae Station
📞	03-6240-9854
🕐	Check-in 4:00 pm – 11:00 pm Check-out 11:00 am
🚫	–

- The lounge space is open all day, from breakfast to evening bar.
- The private rooms are great, but there are also shared spaces where you can meet more people.

Hallway from the front doors ©Mitsumasa Fujitsuka

Take in both nature and art in this refined museum

Omotesando

🚶 Nezu Museum

Even those who don't know much about art can appreciate the beauty of Nezu Museum and its gardens. The building is designed by renowned architect Kengo Kuma. The exhibition spaces and the open green gardens embody traditional Japanese design. The sound of *shishi-odoshi* (a type of bamboo fountain that makes a noise when tipped over by dripping water) resonating through the green space cleanses your mind and soul. After some time with the art, take a break at Nezucafé, where you can admire the deep greenery beyond the windows.

📍 6-5-1, Minami-Aoyama, Minato-ku

🚃 Omotesando Station

📞 03-3400-2536

🕐 10:00 am – 5:00 pm

🚫 Mondays (open if holiday and closed next business day), between exhibitions, New Year's holidays

- The annual zodiac pins make a great souvenir.
- The tea rooms in the garden are available for rent.

Surprising outside, comforting inside

Omotesando

🎁 SunnyHills Minami Aoyama

July 1 is Architect Day in Japan, and you can pay respects right here in Tokyo. Kengo Kuma, who also designed the New National Stadium, is the mastermind behind this store with its pineapple-like exterior. Just what is this place? As you enter, you are surrounded by beams of light streaming through the spaces between the joined wood, engulfing you in a magical forestlike space. And then you realize you're actually standing in a Taiwanese pineapple cake shop.

📍 3-10-20, Minami-Aoyama, Minato-ku

🚌 Omotesando Station

📞 03-3408-7778

🕐 11:00 am – 7:00 pm

🚫 New Year's holidays

- Taiwanese tea and cakes are waiting to be served to you.
- The sweet, ripe pineapple juice is popular.

Architects
are amazing

A beautiful architectural model museum

Tennozu Isle

🚶 Archi-Depot Museum

Next up is Japan's first museum of architectural models. The Kuma Kengo buildings introduced earlier are also archived here. Familiar buildings as well as designs that have never been realized are all before you as miniature models. Some consider architecture the highest form of art; here's an opportunity to see inside the minds of Japan's finest artists.

📍 2-6-10, Higashishinagawa, Shinagawa-ku

🚆 Tennozu Isle Station

📞 03-5769-2133

🕐 11:00 am – 7:00 pm

🚫 Mondays (open if holiday, closed next business day)

• The museum was renovated and reopened in spring 2018.
• If your interest in architecture is piqued, try attending their events and symposiums.

You'll feel posh just being here

la kagū

Photo by: la kagu

A sophisticated shop in a renovated book warehouse

Kagurazaka

Akomeya Tokyo in La Kagu

Converted from Shinchosha Publishing's old warehouse, this spacious building is the flagship location of lifestyle store Akomeya. Their brand concept is "happiness spreads from a fresh bowl of rice," and the store carries over twenty types of rice, rice-related food products, cooking utensils, skin-care products and more. Browse the chic, beautifully designed products then rest and eat at one of the in-house restaurants. The second floor is an event space for workshops organized by Shinchosha.

📍 67, Yaraicho, Shinjuku-ku

🚃 Kagurazaka Station

📞 03-5227-6977

🕐 11:00 am – 8:30 pm
Café 11:00 am – 8:30 pm

🚫 Irregular

• Shiratama Salon Shinsaburo is produced by Shiratamaya Shinsaburo, a 380-year-old *shiratama* specialty shop.
• Don't miss out on the limited products and packaging you can only find at the flagship store.

Like a cloud that melts in your mouth

Shaved natural ice that's sooooo good

Sangenjaya

✗ "Wa" Kitchen Kanna

At Kanna, you can enjoy shaved ice all year round. Using super-clear ice stored at Shogetsu Icehouse, one of six in Japan, it's fluffy and light, and the indulgent sauces are made with seasonal fruits and real milk. Soy-sauce Milk, Strawberry Milk, Kanna's Red Bean and Mochi are all approx. ¥750 each. The secret menu Mascarpone Kiwi Milky Yogurt is delicious, too.

📍 2nd Fl. 2-43-11, Shimouma, Setagaya-ku

🚌 Sangenjaya Station

📞 03-6453-2737

🕚 11:00 am – 7:00 pm
Note: Subject to seasonal change

🚫 Wednesdays

- Premium Milk and Tiramisu also sound amazing.
- Non-dessert meal menus available, too, if you feel like lunch.

Experience the beauty of Edo-style glassware

Photo by: 24trigger_

Sip coffee served in Edo-style glassware

Kinshicho

✘ Sumida Coffee

July 5 is *Kiriko* (Edo-style glasswork) Day. So head over to a café that serves coffee in *kiriko* cups. You'll feel like a star as you drink drip coffee made from fragrant, carefully roasted beans, served from glassware that glitters like a jewel in the light. Pair it with Real Coffee Mocha Cheese Cake. If you want to learn more about the art of *kiriko*, head over to the nearby Sumida Edo Kiriko-kan.

📍 4-7-11, Taihei, Sumida-ku

🚇 Kinshicho Station

📞 03-5637-7783

🕐 11:00 am – 7:00 pm

🚫 Wednesdays, second and fourth Tuesdays of the month (open if holiday, closed next business day)

• Try the famous brick cheese toast.
• Bring home the premium Coffee Liquid as a souvenir.

Delicious and good for you

The salad bar for Salad Anniversary

Ebisu

✗ Cosme Kitchen Adaptation

July 6 is Salad Anniversary, after a line from a famous poem by Machi Tawara, contemporary Japanese writer and poet. With that in mind, it's time for lunch at an exciting salad bar. The restaurant's concept is Clean Eating, and the Clean Eating Buffet (¥2,462) serves a selection of organic, specially grown vegetables, superfoods, and probiotic foods.

📍 2nd Fl. Atré Ebisu, 1-6-1, Ebisuminami, Shibuya-ku

🚉 Ebisu Station

📞 03-5475-8576

🕐 10:00 am – 10:30 pm

🚫 Irregular

- Try their cold-pressed juices.
- The vegan and gluten-free desserts look so good.

Summer illuminations are wonderful, too

A blue Star Festival at Tokyo Tower

Akabanebashi

📷 The Milky Way Illumination

According to legend, deities Orihime and Hikoboshi, separated by the Milky Way, are only allowed to meet once a year on July 7. Put on a *yukata* for a romantic evening at Tokyo Tower to celebrate love tonight. On the first floor of the main deck, the Milky Way Illumination makes its appearance every year (entry fee ¥900). The blue LED lights strewn across the ceiling almost look like the real Milky Way when reflected onto the windows at night. It's tradition to write a wish down and hang it on bamboo for Star Festival. What wish will you make tonight?

📍 4-2-8, Shibakoen, Minato-ku

🚇 Akabanebashi Station

📞 03-3433-5111

🕐 9:00 am - 11:00 pm

🚫 –

- Look for Orihime and Hikoboshi, represented by Vega and Altair, among the stars.
- The outdoor deck area is also decorated and open for viewing.

Wake up early for summer blooms

Iriya

🚶 Iriya Morning Glory Festival

The Iriya Morning Glory Festival starts every year on July 6 and lasts for three days. Along the street are about one hundred Morning Glory traders and one hundred vendor booths. Because morning glories bloom at sunrise, the festival starts at 5:00 am. At dawn, the air is nippy and smells like summer, conjuring thoughts of gardening. Set your alarms, and get out of bed early to see these potted beauties.

📍 1-12-16, Iriya, Taito-ku

🚇 Iriya Station

📞 03-3841-1800

🕐 5:00 am – 11:00 pm

🚫 –

- It's hard to resist buying a potted morning glory.
- Go on, challenge yourself to new gardening resolutions this year.

Even your soul feels refreshed

Visit an elegant, hidden mansion

Takaosanguchi

✗ Ukai Toriyama

Mount Takao is considered one of Tokyo's quiet getaway spots. Deep in the mountains, *Sukiya-zukuri* (a type of vernacular Japanese house) architecture relocated from Toyama has been transformed into a rustic restaurant dedicated to high-class, seasonal charcoal-grilled cuisine. Breathing in the pure mountain air, your worries just slip away. In summer, the lights are sometimes turned off for a magical moment with the dancing fireflies. The ephemeral passing of summer is melancholy and beautiful in this mysterious world.

- 📍 3426, Minamiasakawamachi, Hachioji-shi
- 🚌 Takaosanguchi Station and shuttle bus
- 📞 042-661-0739
- 🕐 11:30 am – 9:30 pm Sundays and holidays: 11:30 am – 9:00 pm
- 🚫 Tuesdays (open during peak season), check website for other days

- The charcoal-grilled chicken course is ¥5,830 (with additional ten percent surcharge).
- In fall, celebrate the full moon here during the Mid-Autumn Festival.

It's bigger than your face!

Mecca of niche and its eight-tiered soft serve

Nakano

✗ Daily Chiko

Nakano Broadway is mecca for collectors and enthusiasts of niche, specialized hobbies. After going on the prowl for that one figure or comic book you've been dying to get your hands on, you'll want to try the notorious eight-tiered soft serve (¥490). Made up of a random mix of eight flavors from vanilla, chocolate, café au lait, strawberry, grape, Hokkaido cantaloupe, *matcha*, *ramune* soda and more, this 16-inch-tall swirling tower of color will drive the kid in you wild. The sheer size of this snack makes it perfect for sharing!

📍 B1, Nakano Broadway, 5-52-15, Nakano, Nakano-ku

🚇 Nakano Station

📞 03-3386-4461

🕐 10:00 am – 8:00 pm

🚫 –

- The *sanuki* udon is another must-try on their menu.
- Nakano Broadway itself is a rabbit hole of cool.

The soft serve you'll want every day of summer

Sendagaya

Laitier

This adorable café was created in homage to rich, fresh milk. *Laitier* is French for milkman, and the milk- and mascarpone-flavored soft serves live up to the name. With toppings like brandy in a dropper, seasonal fruit, nuts, and more, everyone's soft serve is personalized to perfection. The blue walls serve as a beautiful backdrop, too.

- 1st Fl. 1-22-7, Sendagaya, Shibuya-ku
- Sendagaya Station
- 03-6455-5262
- 11:00 am – 7:30 pm
- Tuesdays (open if national holiday)

- Try the 3-Nut and Honey and Milk Soft Serve (¥842).
- Galettes are available for you hungry folk!

A starry sky, even when it's raining

Higashi-Ikebukuro

🚶 Planetarium "Manten"

At the rooftop of Sunshine City in Ikebukuro, the night is always starry. Inside Konica Minolta Planetarium 'Manten,' snuggle into the Cloud Seat sofa for two (¥3,800 per sofa), and the planetarium becomes your own little world. Or try the Lawn Seat (¥3,500 per seat), which allows you to lie down for the viewing. On a hot summer day, an air-conditioned indoor date is just perfect.

📍 Roof, 3-1-3, Higashi-Ikebukuro, Toshima-ku

🚉 Higashi-Ikebukuro Station

📞 03-3989-3546

🕐 11:00 am show – 8:00 pm show
Note: Subject to seasonal change

🚫 Closed for maintenance/ preparation between shows

- Collaboration shows with popular bands like Glay are available.
- Visit the aquarium next door while you're at it.

How tall can it go?

Where the Lemon Sour was invented

Yutenji

✕ Motsuyaki Ban

July 13 is *Motsuyaki* (grilled offal) Day, the perfect time to go to a bar that's fast, cheap, and good. Ban's famous lemon sour is *shochu* (a type of sake) mixed with the original carbonated "sour," with a whole fresh lemon squeezed in. Not too sweet, you just want to knock these back with a few grilled pork offal skewers (¥100 per skewer). Don't forget to see who can stack the taller tower with the left-over lemon peels. It's a challenge when you're buzzed!

📍 2-8-17, Yutenji, Meguro-ku

🚋 Yutenji Station

📞 03-3792-3021

🕐 4:00 pm – 11:00 pm
Saturday: 3:00 pm – 11:00 pm
Sunday: 3:00 pm – 10:00 pm

🚫 Irregular

- The famous offal stew and fried pork liver are must-tries.
- On Tuesday, enjoy free hard-boiled eggs on the house.

There's something about lanterns at night

A wall of light built from 30,000 lanterns

Kudanshita

🚶 Yasukuni Shrine Mitama Matsuri

Yasukuni Shrine is a highlight of summer. The festival takes place every year from July 13 to July 16, and lanterns of all sizes hang along the boulevard—some thirty thousand of them. The big lanterns are hung around the outer gardens. Inside, more lanterns set the *Kudan* area aglow. Anyone can apply to have their name shown on a lantern. Head out in the evening—you don't want to miss this.

📍	3-1-1, Kudankita, Chiyoda-ku
🚇	Kudanshita Station
📞	03-3261-8326
🕐	Prayer times 6:00 am – 9:30 pm
🚫	–

- The earliest *Bon* Dance of Tokyo takes place here.
- Come see the *Aomori Nebuta* floats and *Awa* dances, too.

Raise your glasses, and be merry!

Start at noon and go until morning

Asakusa

✘ Asakusa Hoppy Street

In the middle of the hot, dry summer, come to Asakusa Hoppy Street for a cold one. A string of cheap drinking spots line the streets, making this a perfect place for a catch-up over a few drinks. Tourists, locals, everyone nearby is flushed with happiness, and it's infectious. Not familiar with Hoppy? It's a beer-flavored, low-calorie, low-sugar, barely alcoholic drink that's gentle on your body. Hoppy Street used to be known as Stew Street for its famous beef stews. Try it with some Hoppy!

📍 Near 2-3/4, Asakusa, Taito-ku

🚉 Asakusa Station

📞 Depends on store

🕐 Depends on store

🚫 Depends on store

- Bar hop not just for beer, but for stew.
- While you're here, why not head to the nearby race track and bet on a horse?

You've never seen cake as cheeky as this

Note: This is a seasonal dessert

Wanna chomp on this sexy cake?

Ikejiri-Ohashi

✗ Patisserie La Glycine

This patisserie's specialty is a super-cute peach dessert that looks like a plump bum in a cute bikini evocative of the beach, and it's called Summer Memories (available only during summer). The whole-peach compote is flavored with white wine and whipped cream. There are also ten types of macarons you can choose from to bring home. Ask the macaron-loving patisserie chefs for their recommendations; they know what they're talking about.

📍 1st Fl. 3-17-7, Aobadai, Meguro-ku

🚉 Ikejiri-Ohashi Station

📞 03-6455-0213

🕐 11:00 am – 8:00 pm

🚫 Mondays, third Tuesdays of the month (open if holiday, closed next business day)

- Summer-only shaved ice at a patisserie? Yes please!
- Their eclairs are designed so they're easy to eat while you walk.

Dessert from a jewelry brand!

Desserts you'll want to wear

Omotesando

✗ Q-Pot Cafe.

Q-Pot is a jewelry brand known for its dessert-themed accessories. The café was renovated in the spring of 2018, and the accessories here are just for eating. At the collar of elegant monochrome dresses are colorful, delicious necklaces. The clever, jewelry-like plating is simply enchanting. The interior, too, is cute as a dream, so don't forget to take a photo to commemorate.

📍 3-4-8, Jingumae, Shibuya-ku

🚊 Omotesando Station

📞 03-6447-1218

🕐 11:00 am – 8:00 pm

🚫 New Year's holidays

- If you're a fan of Q-Pot, wear your favorite piece when you go.
- Anyone can feel like a princess here!

There's something comforting about dusk and the sea

Photo by: MC/PIXTA

Take a breath with a summer sunset over Mount Fuji

Tateyama

📷 Sunset at Hojo Beach

If you're feeling overwhelmed and need to rest and recharge, this is the perfect place to do it. The sun colors everything in sight a vibrant orange before sinking into the sea at Hojo Beach, also known as Mirror Bay for its calm and gentle waters. Your anxiety will melt at the sound of the incoming waves, and your worries wash away with the outgoing tide. The scenery here is waiting to embrace you.

📍 Hojo, Tateyama-shi, Chiba

🚇 Tateyama Station

📞 0470-22-2544
(Tateyama City Tourism Office)

🕐 24 hours

🚫 –

• A three-minute walk from the station for those on foot and free parking if you drive.
• Diamond Fuji, when the sun aligns with the peak of Mount Fuji, can be seen in mid-May and late July.

The view of
a lifetime

Photo by: Oi/PIXTA

Sunrise at Mount Fuji is bucket list material

🚶 Mount Fuji

If someone says "Japan," one of the first places that springs to mind is Mount Fuji. Its popularity skyrocketed since it was added to the World Heritage List as a Cultural Site in 2013. The popular Yoshida Trail is only open from July to September, but two hundred fifty thousand people pass through the trail every year. The sunrise from the peak is on a lot of bucket lists. The harder the climb, the greater the reward, and you'll believe it when you see it for yourself. The weather changes quickly up there, so prepare with warm and waterproof clothing.

📍 –

🚆 –

📞 –

🕐 –

🚫 *Note: Please see the official website for more information*

- The view from the top is breathtaking.
- A cup of instant noodles would go perfectly with this scenery.

Beat the heat with crispy-on-the-outside, tender-on-the-inside eel

Azabu-Juban

Azabu-Juban Eel Hanabusa

The tradition of eating eel to fight summer fatigue originated in the Edo period, when people would eat eel approximately eighteen days before the changing of seasons. Hanabusa Tokyo does not prepare their eel *edoyaki*-style, which involves steaming the eel before grilling it. Instead, the *jiyaki*-style eel is grilled directly, preserving its natural texture. Enjoy it served traditionally on a bowl of rice, or try the Nagoya-style *Hitsumabushi*, where the eel is sliced and placed over a pot of rice, to be moved into a separate serving bowl before eating.

- 5th Fl. 2-8-8, Azabu-Juban, Minato-ku
- Azabujuban Station
- 03-3457-5870
- 11:30 am - 2:30 pm
  5:30 pm - 9:30 pm
- Irregular

- Smack your lips at the premium Aichi-bred eel.
- If it's too busy, try the Shibuya location with double the seats.

Chilled noodle season's back!

Get a taste of summer in the place where chilled ramen was invented

Jimbocho

🍴 Yosukosaikan

Chilled Ramen is a Japanese summer staple, and it was started here in Tokyo. Established in 1906, this long-standing Chinese restaurant's signature summer dish is Mixed Cold Noodles, and its traditional sweet and sour flavors are spot on. Colorful toppings that represent the four seasons are piled impressively high in the shape of Mount Fuji. Slurp up those noodles and survive the summer heat! (Ooh, will you look at that? Two meatballs are hidden inside!)

📍 1-11-3, Jimbocho, Kanda, Chiyoda-ku

🚉 Jimbocho Station

📞 03-3291-0218

🕐 11:30 am – 9:30 pm

🚫 New Year's holidays

- Try another dish they brought to Japan, the Spicy Seafood Soup Noodles.
- Try famous Japanese author Shōtarō Ikenami's favorite, Shanghai Chowmein.

The most relaxed way to camp!

Photo by: Shimokita Terrace

Tokyo glamping in Shimokitazawa

Shimokitazawa

🚶 Shimokita Terrace

It's summer, and you want to go on a camping trip somewhere out of the city, but can't find time to leave town...fear not! The Shimokitazawa glamping experience is the perfect compromise. Climb to the rooftop of the building and feel your heart flutter at the sight of the cityscape and the enormous tent. Barbecue sets and tools are available, so you can show up empty-handed. The space is available for groups of ten to forty people. The trendiest party of the summer is right at your fingertips! (Starts at ¥4,298 for two hours, reservation required.)

📍 2-34-3, Kitazawa, Setagaya-ku

🚉 Shimokitazawa Station

📞 03-6427-5800

🕐 10:00 am – 11:00 pm

🚫 New Year's holidays

- Additional services like the incredible Champagne Tower are available.
- Surprisingly, you are free to bring your own drinks!

23

A metropolitan outdoor BBQ... that's luxury!

Barbecue in Tokyo? Gotta be here

Shin-Toyosu

🚶 Wild Magic

Feel like inviting the new friends you met in Tokyo out for some barbecue? Come to Wild Magic. Step onto camp grounds and you'll be greeted by teepee-style tents and even trailer homes. In this surprisingly foreign "American" space, feast on juicy sirloin steak and even roast some marshmallows afterward (¥5,400/person for the Standard BBQ Course). The best part is that you can show up and leave empty-handed!

📍 6-1-23, Toyosu, Koto-ku

🚉 Shin-Toyosu Station

📞 –

🕐 10:00 am – 10:00 pm
Note: Barbecue area is available in four-hour intervals

🚫 Irregular

• Take a photo in front of the white tents.
• Try some Mexican chimichangas for dessert.

Tomari Beach, Shikinejima / Photo by: Shikinejima Tourist Office

The islands just 2.5 hours away

Takeshiba

🚶 Niijima and Shikinejima

Did you know about Tokyo's islands? They're about ninety-nine miles to the south. You can get to this Pacific paradise in two and a half hours by speedboat, or thirty-five minutes by plane from Chofu if you're headed to Niijima. You'll feel like you've arrived in a Caribbean oasis! Spend all day on the beach or in the shops and museums on Niijima. At night, gorge on seafood at a sushi restaurant. On Shikinejima, three open-air hot springs are open twenty-four hours a day. Gaze out to sea and relish the good vibes. This trip will satisfy all of your senses.

📍 Niijima, Niijima/Shikinejima

🚇 Takeshiba Station and 2.5 hours by speedboat

📞 04992-5-0240 (Niijima Ward Office)

🕐 Please check the official site for ferry schedule

🚫 –

- It's a ten-minute ride between the two islands on the Nishiki ferry.
- Turn off your phone and detox from the digital world.

Sun and sea
on a day trip
from the city

The clearest waters in Tokyo! Start your summer here

Kazusaokitsu

⭑ Moriya Beach

An hour and a half on the express train from Tokyo station, and you're by the ocean, baby! The crystal-clear waters of Katsuura are some of the most limpid in the Kanto area. No complaints here—the waves are gentle, the parking lot close, and public showers are available. The abundant seaweed is part of the charm. This beach is safe for the whole family. It does get crowded on weekends, so you'll want to arrive early. The way there and back is part of the fun, so treasure every summer moment.

📍 Moriya, Katsuura-shi, Chiba

🚃 Kazusaokitsu Station

📞 0470-73-6641
(Katsuura City Tourism Office)

🕐 Check the official website
for times

🚫 –

• Try the Katsuura Tan Tan Noodles at the beachside restaurants.
• Walk to Watajima, or the small island in the inlet, to see the red torii gates.

A chill place for a summer date

Cool off in a natural limestone cave

Okutama

🚶 Nippara Limestone Cave

On a day when you can't get enough AC, this cave is perfect. One of Tokyo's natural monuments, it's easy to access—just walk in (¥700 for entry) and bask in the cool air; the cave's average temperature is about 52°F year round. It cools you down as soon as you enter. Once a mecca for *shugendo* (a Japanese syncretic religion) practitioners, the limestone cave is partially illuminated, reminiscent of a dungeon from a fantasy world. Did you know that it takes about one hundred years for the limestone to grow half an inch? As you explore, be awed by the power of time.

📍 1052, Nippara, Okutamamachi, Nishitamagun

🚌 Okutama Station and bus

📞 0428-83-8491

🕐 Apr. 1 – Nov. 30: 8:00 am – 5:00 pm
Dec. 1 – Mar. 31: 8:30 am – 4:30 pm

🚫 New Year's holidays

- Try the salted grilled fish at the shop.
- You can go fishing at the nearby Nippara River.

Spend an indulgent night right here

The resort pool with a view of the Rainbow Bridge

Daiba

🏨 Grand Nikko Tokyo Daiba

While you're in Tokyo this summer, grab your friends and spend the evening in Grand Blue, the outdoor pool of this urban resort. Float around with the Rainbow Bridge and Tokyo Tower as your backdrop. Take in the view of Tokyo's city lights glimmering over the sea at night from this summer-only terrace pool. A liberating summer night in the open spaces of Daiba... what will it bring for you?

📍 2-6-1, Odaiba, Minato-ku

🚃 Daiba Station

📞 03-5500-6750

🕐 Terrace pool only open during summer—please check the official website for details

🚫 –

• The panoramic view of Tokyo Bay is breathtaking.
• How about a luxurious dinner with a night view at the hotel restaurant?

The *Tokyo Fireworks Show*

Asakusa/Kuramae

📷 Sumida River Fireworks Show

Fireworks are a part of many countries' annual festivities. This is the largest fireworks show in Tokyo, and you've never seen anything like it. Will you climb Skytree to watch from above? Or will you go to Shioiri Park and try for a photograph of Skytree lit up by fireworks? Or maybe somewhere calmer, like inside Asakusa Temple? You can even avoid the crowd by taking a cruise in Tokyo Bay for a view from the sea. The choice is yours. Find your own way to enjoy these fireworks.

📍 Sumida River, Lower Sakurabashi to Upper Kototoibashi (First Area) Lower Komagatabashi to Upper Umayabashi (Second Area)

🚆 Asakusa Station (First Area) Kuramae Station (Second Area)

📞 03-5608-1111

🕐 Please check the official website

🚫 –

• The show is held annually in July.
• Book a hotel room that faces the fireworks.

> Stars so
> wondrous you
> might well cry

Photo by: rontioriginal/PIXTA

Be moved by a sky full of stars

Okutama

📷 Lake Okutama

Amid the complexity of life, sometimes you need to stop, look up, and take in the vastness of the universe. When you need that break, hop in your car in the middle of the night and drive to Lake Okutama. In fact, this is one of Tokyo's best spots for stargazing. When you arrive at Lake Okutama Dam Site Parking, open the doors and peer at the sky. Up there for you is a silent, all-embracing night of falling stars.

📍 Hara, Okutamamachi, Nishitamagun

🚌 Okutama Station and bus

📞 0428-83-2152 (Okutamamachi Tourist Information Center)

🕐 24 hours

🚫 –

- Another spot is Tsukiyomi Parking Lot No. 2.
- During the day, visit the beautiful Hatonosu Valley.

The restaurant of blue skies and blue seas on the Miura Peninsula

Zushi

🍴 Marine & Farm Sajima

The concept and motto of Marine & Farm is "Eat Locally." Sit back on the crisp, white seats on the ocean-view terrace, and tuck into delicious dishes made from ingredients sourced from Sajima and the Miura Peninsula. Beyond the crystal-clear sea waters, you can see Mount Fuji in the distance. The scenery at dusk is so out of this world, you'll forget you're only on a day trip out of Tokyo.

📍 3-8-35, Sajima, Yokosuka-shi, Kanagawa

🚆 Zushi Station and bus

📞 046-854-9820

🕐 11:00 am – 9:00 pm
Weekends and holidays:
9:00 am – 9:00 pm

🚫 Irregular

• The Napoli pizza and pasta using seafood from the Miura Peninsula are amazing.
• Even their vegetables are super fresh.

A taste of America's west coast in Tokyo

Try their finest craft beer on a seaside terrace

Tennozu Isle

✗ T.Y. Harbor

This brewery restaurant was renovated from an old post-war warehouse. From the mild pale ales to the fruity wheat ale, you can taste the love they've poured into the craft beer that's brewed in-house (starts from ¥580 for a small). The beers pair beautifully with American cuisine such as burgers or steak. It's hard to believe you're in Tokyo when the canal-facing terrace seems to slow the fast pace of the city.

📍 2-1-3, Higashi-Shinagawa, Shinagawa-ku

🚈 Tennozu Isle Station

📞 03-5479-4555

🕐 Lunch: 11:30 am – 2:00 pm
Weekends and holidays:
11:30 am – 3:00 pm
Dinner: 5:30 pm – 10:00 pm

🚫 –

• The floating River Lounge is available by reservation.
• Vegetarians rejoice, there are plenty of meat-free options on the menu.

Cool down with elegance

Relief from the heat sitting over a river

Shuzenji

✗ Yugashima Tatsuta Ryokan

Enjoying the breeze on a *kawatoko* (a terrace built beside or over a river) isn't reserved for Kyoto's Kamo River—Tokyo has its own in the Izu and Hakone area, with jetty seats. The view of Nekko River's powerful waters and its musical roar set the mood for an atmospheric dinner. The private hot spring in a bamboo grove is illuminated at night, just to elevate your evening even further.

📍 347, Yugashima, Izu-shi, Shizuoka

🚆 Shuzenji Station and bus

📞 0558-85-0511

🕐 Check-in 3:00 pm – 6:00 pm
Check-out 10:00 am

🚫 –

- Enjoy a feast of local produce on the *kawatoko*.
- Roll in the hammocks on the river-top terrace.

What is this white mousse?

Photo by: enjoyfeedme

White curry udon like a savory soft serve

Ebisu

✗ Shodai

August 2 is Curry Udon Day. Today, you'll want to try the expectation-defying curry udon noodles. Shodai's White Curry Udon looks just like a bowl of vanilla soft serve! In reality, it's a fluffy white potato foam; a special sauce made by foaming a combination of broth and steamed potatoes. Poke around inside and you'll discover spicy, curry-covered udon noodles. Incredible! Best paired with some sake.

📍 1st Fl. 1-1-10, Ebisuminami, Shibuya-ku

🚉 Ebisu Station

📞 03-3714-7733

🕐 5:00 pm – 3:00 am
Sundays and holidays
(excluding before long holiday):
5:00 pm – 12:00 am

🚫 –

- They're open until 4:00 am, a perfect meal for sobering up after a long night out.
- Also available at its sister store, Roji, in Mizonokuchi.

Personalized nuts in honey!

Start a honey obsession here

Meiji-Jingumae <Harajuku>

My Honey Omotesando

August 3 is the Day of Honey. It's yummy, good for you, pretty to look at, and never spoils. At this store, you can combine your choice of nuts and honey to make My Honey (sold by weight). Pair honey-soaked nuts with yogurt as a part of your breakfast, have a little spoonful as a snack at noon, and pamper your hair with honey shampoo in the evening. Speak with a honey beauty adviser for tips on working honey into your daily routine for a healthier life.

📍 4-23-6, Jingumae, Shibuya-ku

🚇 Meiji-Jingumae <Harajuku> Station

📞 03-3470-8352

🕐 11:00 am – 8:00 pm

🚫 Mondays

- Try the Honey Cordial Syrup, which you can put in beer.
- Try the honey cocoa chocolate, too.

August

4

It's like walking on water!

Go for a summer drive seeking the thrilling and the breathtaking

Senzu

📷 Yume no Tsuribashi Bridge

It's time for adventure! August 4 is Suspension Bridge Day, and what better destination than the beautiful Sumatakyo Gorge in Shizuoka? Challenge yourself with tunnels and steep steps on the walk from Sumatakyo Hot Springs, and emerge before a stunning scene of an emerald river and lively greenery. Hanging twenty-five feet above is a 295-foot-long bridge that's only two planks wide. Legend has it if you make a wish about someone you are fond of in the middle of the bridge, it will come true!

📍 Sumatakyo, Senzu, Kawanehoncho, Haibaragun, Shizuoka

🚃 Senzu Station and bus

📞 0547-59-2746

🕐 24 hours
(daytime is recommended)

🚫 –

- Cross with someone you've been flirting with.
- Catch the steam engine trains still operating nearby.

Who knew goldfish were so pretty?

Note: Photo from the 2017 exhibit

The swimming, breathing aquarium art here is lit up like Vegas

Mitsukoshimae

🚶 Art Aquarium

The Art Aquarium exhibit has been an annual show at the Nihonbashi Mitsui Hall since 2011. In the dimly lit exhibition hall is a glittering world of lights, brilliant like a sleepless city night. The exhibition's theme and content changes every year, mesmerizing people with countless goldfish and one-of-a-kind aquariums built in collaboration with traditional Japanese craftsmen (entry fee approx. ¥1,000). A great place to cool down in summer and be intoxicated by a beautiful fantasy.

📍 5th Fl. Coredo Muromachi 1 (entrance on 4th Fl.), 2-2-1, Muromachi, Nihonbashi, Chuo-ku, Tokyo

🚇 Mitsukoshimae Station

📞 Check official website

🕐 Check official website

🚫 –

- Takes place annually between early July to late September.
- Attend events such as live DJ performances.

I can't believe it's really candy!

Edible art crafted with bare hands and a pair of scissors

Tokyo Skytree

🎁 Asakusa Amezaiku Ame-Shin

This goldfish isn't made of glass...it's candy. Fortune cats, shiba inu, eagles, Pegasus...they make them all. *Amezaiku* is traditional Japanese candy crafting, and these crystalline works of art are made by skillfully sculpting hot melted sugar by hand. At the Skytree location, you can watch craftsmen create these beautiful edible sculptures right before you. At the Asakusa main branch, hands-on workshops are available. These would be such a waste to eat!

📍 Inside Soramachi, Tokyo Skytree Town, 1-1-2, Oshiage, Sumida-ku

🚊 Tokyo Skytree Station

📞 03-5808-7988

🕐 10:00 am – 9:00 pm

🚫 Same as Skytree Town

- Bring home some candy syrup to put on your toast.
- Custom candy sculpting requests are available.

Expires in 20 minutes? That's bananas!

Sugar-free, flavor-filled, super-rich banana juice

Hatchobori

✗ Sonna Banana

The owner really saw the a-peel of his post-drinking session banana juice...so much that he ended up selling them! That's bananas, right!? Jokes and puns aside, you can really taste the love in each cup. The only ingredients in this superjuice are bananas and milk. No sugar, no embellishments. It's not only tasty, it may even help with issues such as swelling and irregular bowel movements. The best choice for Banana (8=*ba*, 7=*nana*) Day.

📍 1st Fl. 2-15-5, Hatchobori, Chuo-ku

🚇 Hatchobori Station

📞 080-3707-0877

🕐 8:00 am – 9:15 am
11:00 am – 7:00 pm
Saturday: 11:00 am – 5:00 pm

🚫 Sundays, national holidays

- Try the *uji matcha*, cocoa, or *kinako* (sweet roasted soy powder) mix.
- These are great even if you're on a calorie budget.

Rainbow Bagel!

The famous Rainbow Bagel from NYC

Azabu-Juban

✗ New New York Club

Get the latest bakery trend from NYC right here, at New New York Club Bagel and Sandwich Shop. You'll want to ask for Rainbow Colored at the Azabu-Juban branch. This psychedelic cream cheese treat is the talk of the town. If you're at the Jiyugaoka location, don't forget to try food stall favorite Chicken over Rice. By the way, did you know August 8 is Bagel Day in Japan?

📍 3-8-5 Azabu-Juban, Minato-ku

🚇 Azabu-Juban Station

📞 03-6873-1537

🕐 9:00 am – 6:00 pm
(or until sold out)

🚫 Check website

• Rainbow Colored is only available on weekends and holidays.
• Give the vivid Pink Flamingo a try, too.

This pool feels like a nightclub!

Be liberated by a pool of vibrant lights and colors

Akasakamitsuke

🏨 The New Otani

With a Japanese garden about ten acres wide and a rotating lounge on the top floor, The New Otani is one of the top executive hotels in Tokyo. Its brilliantly illuminated nighttime pool is exceptional. The first thing you'll want to do is sit in one of the private seating areas and raise your champagne glass. After that, give yourself over to the live DJ performance. Tonight, treat yourself like a celebrity—free to do whatever you like, however you want. Don't hold back!

📍 4-1, Kioicho, Chiyoda-ku

🚇 Akasakamitsuke Station

📞 03-3265-1111

🕐 Check website

🚫 –

- Open annually from July to September.
- There are only ten private seating areas.

Spend all weekend in this hotel

Tateyama

🏨 Opa Village

August 10 is the Day of Hearts. Cannonball into a heart-shaped pool in Chiba's resort central, the Boso Peninsula. The resort is built in the image of a rural town in southern France, and after you check in, relax by the pool until sunset. There are plenty of places and activities to indulge in: the hammocks in the garden, delicious French cuisine made from locally sourced ingredients, private wine baths... This weekend, spend a night tending to your heart at this vacation-home hotel.

📍 1687, Inuishi, Tateyama-shi, Chiba

🚌 Tateyama Station and bus

📞 0470-28-1000

🕐 Check-in: 3:00 pm – 10:00 pm
Check-out: 11:00 am

🚫 Irregular

• There is a hotel library, so grab a book to read by the pool.
• The citrus bath, with locally picked fruit floating in it, is heavenly.

Looks like a scene from a movie, doesn't it?

At the end of the lane is one of the top 100 beaches of the world

Zushi

🚶 Isshiki Beach

There are only two weeks of summer left, so let's hit the beach! The path leads to one of CNN's "100 best beaches around the world." You must see the outstandingly beautiful waters and stunning crescent-shaped sands with your own eyes. You can even see Mount Fuji from here. The waters are shallow enough for kids to play safely, and it's less crowded here than the Shonan beaches. For those of you who want some breathing room, we recommend Isshiki Beach.

📍	Beyond 2123, Isshiki, Hayamacho, Miuragun, Kanagawa
🚆	Zushi Station and bus
📞	046-876-1111 (Hayama Economy Promotion Division)
🕐	–
🚫	–

• Take a romantic, cinema-esque picture on the path to the beach.
• Stop by The Museum of Modern Art, Kamakura & Hayama.

Can't help but hum "Surfin' USA"...

Beach time with the family in a secret spot

Chigasaki

🚶 Southern Beach Chigasaki

Teeming with surfers in the early mornings, this captivating spot gives you a view of Mount Fuji at the end of the stretches of sand. The beach is not the only place named after the rock band Southern All Stars, who are originally from Chigasaki. After fun on the beach, take a stroll around town, where you'll find places like Southern Shopping Street and Southern Shrine. Wash off at the hot springs at the end of the day, and wrap up your fulfilling Shonan vacation. Don't forget to commemorate the trip by the photo spot Chigasaki Southern C.

📍 4-4-12986, Nakakaigan, Chigasaki-shi, Kanagawa

🚉 Chigasaki and bus

📞 0467-88-5981 (line open only during beach season)

🕐 Open for swimming 8:30 am – 5:00 pm

🚫 –

• The beach is open for swimming from the first Saturday of July until August 31.
• Check out the sunset by the hat-shaped Eboshi Rock.

Try the Kitaro menu!

© Mizukipro

How about some Daddy Eyeball Chestnut Zenzai?

Chofu

✗ Kitaro Tea House

As you might know, in Japan, summer is the spooky season. When it comes to Japanese ghosts and monsters, popular manga character Kitaro can't be beaten. Kitaro's creator spent part of his life in Chofu, and the town is filled with "ghosts." At this tea house, you can find Kitaro's home in the trees, a Wally Wall bench—the entire building is a world of monsters. Fun desserts like Daddy Eyeball Chestnut *Zenzai* (¥600) or Rollo Cloth's Tea House Sundae (¥800) are a must-have.

📍 5-12-8, Jindaijimotomachi, Chofu-shi

🚌 Chofu Station and bus

📞 042-482-4059

🕐 10:00 am – 5:00 pm

🚫 Mondays (open if holiday, closed next business day)

- Pick up some limited merchandise or Shigeru Mizuki's books.
- Check out Shigeru Mizuki's *yokai* (Japanese spirit monsters) art in the gallery.

August

14

Feel like a bite?

Visit a **VAMPIRE CAFE**

Ginza

✕ VAMPIRE CAFE

Sink your teeth into the macabre with dinner and drinks at this popular vampire-themed café in Ginza. Immortal creatures of the night serve delicious cocktails like the *Nosferatu* and eye-catching dishes such as *The Executed Body of Van Helsing*. The creepy atmosphere of this gothic paradise will ensure you have an unforgettable night!

📍 Rapebiru 7F, 6-7-6, Ginza

🚇 Ginza Station

📞 03-3289-5360

🕐 5:00 pm – 11:30 pm

🚫 New Year's holidays
(Please check the official website)

- A cover charge applies.
- Reservations recommended.

A beer garden with a view!

A beer garden to visit by cableway

Takaosanguchi

✕ Mount Takao Beermount

Knocking one back while looking out over the world—is this heaven? This beer garden is open from June to October on the observation deck next to Takaosan Cableway Station. At an elevation of 1,640 feet, the deck gives you a full view of the Kanto area, from Tokyo all the way to Yokohama. The beer here somehow just tastes better. With over three million hikers every year, Mount Takao is the most climbed mountain in the world. It even has three stars in the *Michelin Guide*!

📍 2205, Takaocho, Hachioji-shi

🚃 Takaosanguchi Station

📞 042-665-9943

🕐 Check official website

🚫 –

- Try all six beers available.
- Keep your eyes peeled for seasonal events such as the Star Festival or Mid-Autumn Festival.

Can you believe this view is free?

Photo by: kawamura_lucy/PIXTA

Be intoxicated by the night vista

Tochomae

📷 Tokyo Metropolitan Government Office Building

Refresh your body and mind with this captivating night view. For a free view of Tokyo's cityscape, this government office building in Shinjuku is the business. There are observation rooms in both the north and south towers, with the popular Good View Tokyo restaurant on the north side. The high-rise buildings make for a spectacular sight, and the glittering lights that extend beyond the horizon are oh-so-romantic.

- Open until 11:00 pm for the night owls.
- Definitely stop by Good View Tokyo.

📍 2-8-1, Nishi-Shinjuku, Shinjuku-ku

🚃 Tochomae Station

📞 03-5320-7890 (Observation Room)

🕐 9:30 am – 11:00 pm
(North Observation Room)

🚫 First and third Tuesday (South Tower), second and fourth Monday (North Tower), New Year's holidays (excluding Jan. 1), maintenance days

There's something serene about outdoor movies

On a midsummer night, have a good cry under the stars at a cinematic classic

Ebisu

🚶 Picnic Cinema Ebisu

Every year, as a part of a series of events called the Ebisu Garden Picnic, a midsummer night's outdoor film event takes place in Ebisu Garden Place. Artificial turf is laid down in the plaza and a massive screen is set up. A different film is shown every day, and you'll be glad to know you can enjoy them for free. During the day, other events like Picnic Yoga and live music are here to entertain as well.

📍 4-20, Ebisu, Shibuya-ku

🚃 Ebisu Station

📞 03-5423-7111 (Ebisu Garden Place)

🕐 Check website

🚫 –

• Relax on the turf, or grab a chair.
• After the film, how about dinner in Ebisu Garden Place?

Live summer to the fullest at a festival!

The sweatiest day of summer is here

Kaihinmakuhari

🚶 Summer Sonic

For music lovers in Tokyo in August, Summer Sonic is a must. Held simultaneously in Chiba and Osaka, this music festival's electrifying line-up ranges from the hottest J-Pop artists to Billboard-topping performers from the West. The all-night event Sonic Mania opens the festival. Don't miss the chance to party at Japan's greatest summer festival! Hosted annually in mid-August.

📍 1, Mihama, Mihama-ku, Chiba-shi, Chiba

🚇 Kaihinmakuhari Station

📞 –

🕐 Please check the official website

🚫 –

• Sonicvegas and the Stand-Up Show are a good time, too.
• Also, check for details of the annual autograph events.

Get a real taste of Tokyo on a boat

Hop on a houseboat for a river tour of Tokyo's most famous spots

Shinagawa

🚶 Yakatabune Cruiser Funasei

Have you ever seen a *yakatabune*, a Japanese houseboat, and thought to yourself, "I've always wanted to ride one of those!"? This elegant houseboat experience, complete with food and drink, is perfect for taking a tour of Tokyo by water. Charter your own boat for a large group, or share the cruise with other passengers. After you depart from Shinagawa, the cruise takes you under Rainbow Bridge, then past Tokyo Skytree. Last but not least, sail by Daiba on your way back from this two-hour, forty-five-minute journey around Tokyo.

📍 1-16-8, Kita-Shinagawa, Shinagawa-ku

🚃 Shinagawa Station

📞 03-5479-2731

🕐 Check official website

🚫 —

- The cruise is ideal for celebrating birthdays or anniversaries.
- Cruiser yachts are also available for charter.

Ring-a-ling!

Refresh your body and soul with Edo-style wind chimes

Honkawagoe

🚶 Kawagoe Hikawa Shrine

Ring! The sound of glass wind chimes evokes a sense of Japanese summer nostalgia. Every year between July and September, over two thousand Edo-style wind chimes sing for the crowd, and it's truly a feast for your eyes and ears. Other attractions include the River of Light, where the small stream running through the shrine grounds is illuminated, and the super cute *Koi Akari* ("love light") lanterns, which fit perfectly in the palm of your hand (available between August and September). Show up in a *yukata* for the complete experience.

📍 2-11-3, Miyashitamachi, Kawagoe-shi, Saitama

🚉 Honkawagoe Station and bus

📞 049-224-0589

🕐 Hall of wind chimes
9:00 am - 9:00 pm

🚫 Wednesdays (open if national holiday)

• Try the lovable wind chime-shaped desserts at Musubi Café.
• The town of Kawagoe is full of other fun sights.

You'll love having a villa all to yourself

A luxurious vacation at a rental villa in Hayama

Zushi

🏰 The House

You're not imagining it—you really do get this incredible place all to yourself. Here in Hayama, well-known for its high-class villas, these Pacific-facing villas are limited to one rental a day. Terrace jacuzzis, glass-facade dining rooms, bedrooms with a built-in theater (note: projector is extra)...this private getaway is flawless. Splurge a little and treat yourself and your loved ones to some well-deserved alone time. (Contact The House for prices.)

📍 2400-7, Isshiki, Hayamacho, Miuragun, Kanagawa

🚃 Zushi Station and bus

📞 –

🕐 Check-in 2:00 pm
Check-out 10:00 am

🚫 –

- Personal chefs are available for hire.
- Brand-name amenities are available.

These colorful shells are so cute!

Feel like a mermaid at this Enoshima-facing café

Katase-Enoshima

✕ Lucky Meal Mermaid

A restaurant looking out on the picturesque island of Enoshima. Embraced by the Shonan sea breeze, enjoy the resort-like summer vibes right here. The star of the show is the remarkably cute mermaid menu. The Mermaid Spaghetti, decorated with colorful shells, is made with fresh pasta, noble scallop and cabbage, tossed in a pepperoncino sauce. Other enticing dishes such as the Mermaid Baked Risotto, Mermaid Clam Chowder, and more will make it hard for you to choose just one.

📍 2nd Fl. Katase-Kaigan, Fujisawa-shi, Kanagawa

🚈 Katase-Enoshima Station

📞 0466-77-7429

🕐 9:00 am – 9:30 pm
Lunchtime: 11:00 am – 3:00 pm

🚫 –

• Freshly baked bread made with natural *kodama* yeast is a must.
• The floral smoothie cocktails are so photo-worthy.

The shows vary according to time and season

The digital evolution of aquariums

Shinagawa

⮡ Maxell Aqua Park Shinagawa

Come to Aqua Park for a show where dolphins dance through rainbows. You'll want to give a standing ovation to the performance, which includes curtains of water, beams of light, and lovable dolphins prancing and jumping between them. Be awed by projection mapping and the touchscreen-equipped tanks, squeal in delight at penguins or river otters chowing down during feeding time, and enjoy everything the park has to offer. Entry fee is ¥2,200 for adults (anyone over high-school age).

📍 4-10-30, Takanawa, Minato-ku
(inside Shinagawa Prince Hotel)

🚉 Shinagawa Station

📞 03-5421-1111 (automated)

🕐 10:00 am – 10:00 pm
Note: Subject to seasonal change

🚫 –

- Ever been to an aquarium with a merry-go-around inside?
- The café-bar with glowing coral is beautiful.

Look at me, it looks like I'm flying!

The penguins fly at the aquarium in Ikebukuro

Ikebukuro

🚶 Sunshine Aquarium

This aquarium underwent a large-scale renovation, and its new concept is "An Oasis in the Sky." Here you can see flightless penguins swimming overhead, surrounded by jellyfish in an underwater tunnel. See seals swim above you in the donut-shaped pool, and be amazed by other creative displays. The location is easily accessible, so do swing by sometime.

📍 3-1, Higashi-Ikebukuro, Toshima-ku

🚇 Ikebukuro Station

📞 03-3989-3466

🕐 Apr. to Oct. 10:00 am – 8:00 pm
Nov. to Mar. 10:00 am – 6:00 pm

🚫 –

• Get up close and personal with seals at their performance show.
• The outdoor aquarium looks amazing lit up at night.

Oh, wow, look at those juices

The brand-new, bun-free burger

Kinshicho

✗ Shake Tree Burger & Bar

Summer heat getting you down? Energize yourself with some protein! Shake Tree's Wild Out offers a new take on burgers: in place of the buns are 8.5 oz. of beef patty, heartily sandwiching tomato, onions, and cheddar cheese. The fat dripping from the perfectly charred meat is just irresistible. One big bite, and the burger juices and melted cheese will take you to heaven.

📍 1st Fl. 3-13-6, Kamezawa, Sumida-ku

🚇 Kinshicho Station

📞 03-6658-8771

🕐 11:00 am – 3:00 pm
5:00 pm – 9:00 pm
Saturdays: 11:00 am – 9:00 pm
Sundays and holidays:
11:00 am – 5:00 pm

🚫 Mondays (open if holiday, closed next business day)

- Buns are still available for those with more traditional tastes.
- New York-style party menus are available, too!

It looks soooooo spicy!

Can you finish without saying the word "hot"? Try the amazing Soupless Hot Pot.

Ebisu

✗ Nakamura Gen

Now this is a hole-in-the-wall! You'd never know there's a Chinese restaurant inside just from looking at the building. Marked only by a small sign on the second floor, inside you'll find an exotic red counter and a room of people sweating from the spectacular, spicy cuisine. Their signature dish is the *Mala* (Chinese spicy and numbing sauce) Hot Pot. Filled with over fifteen types of deep-fried seasonal veggies, including the medicinal wild rice stem, this "soupless hot pot" is stir-fried with a generous amount of hot peppers and an original hot pot sauce.

📍 1-18-11-201, Ebisuminami, Shibuya-ku

🚃 Ebisu Station

📞 03-3711-5897

🕐 6:00 pm – 11:00 pm
Weekends: 6:00 pm – 10:00 pm

🚫 –

• The party course with all-you-can-eat coriander sounds enticing.
• The Drunken Shrimp, pickled with shaoxing wine, is a must-have.

You'll want to eat these forever!

A gelato shop by a chocolatier

Kagurazaka

✗ Gelateria Theobroma

August 27 is Gelato Day, so it's the perfect time to get some of the real deal. At popular chocolatier Theobroma's gelato shop, you'll want to try their freshly prepped gelato (¥615 for a single scoop) or the Spiral (¥723), a swirl of gelato and fruit. They're so pretty, you might feel conflicted about eating them. The extravagant architecture makes you feel as if you're in an Italian alleyway. Note: the prices listed are for takeout.

📍 Borgo Oojime, 6-8, Kagurazaka, Shinjuku-ku

🚊 Kagurazaka Station

📞 03-5206-5195

🕐 10:30 am – 7:30 pm

🚫 New Year's holidays

- Take a stylish photo in the alley.
- Try the seasonal original parfaits.

Whoa whoa whoa!

Photo by: @ohira_yuki

Nagashi somen *in Kita-Kamakura*

Kita-Kamakura

✕ Chaya-Kado

A stand-alone shop in Kita-Kamakura. Try the Japanese summer classic, *nagashi somen* (literally "flowing *somen*," or thin wheat noodles), in a refined space spattered with elegant sunbeams. After you order the set menu with grated yam and tempura, grab your dipping sauce in one hand, chopsticks in the other. Now, all that's left is to catch the *somen* as they flow by on bamboo tracks. Each ball of noodles is carefully prepared to be an exact mouthful. It's a sociable place where it's easy to strike up a conversation with your neighbors.

📍 1518, Yamanouchi, Kamakura-shi, Kanagawa

🚉 Kita-Kamakura Station

📞 0467-23-1673

🕐 10:00 am – 5:00 pm

🚫 –

- *Nagashi somen* is available from end of March to end of October.
- Take a walk around the temples of Kita-Kamakura while your food settles.

A great place to take a new profile pic for summer

You'll feel like a kid again in this field of sunflowers

Kiyose

📷 Kiyose Sunflower Field

Can't let summer end without visiting a sunflower field, right? It's time to hit the Kiyose Sunflower Festival. Over one hundred thousand sunflowers give the impression of a dazzling collection of stars. It's hard to believe you're still in Tokyo. The sunflowers are in full bloom from mid- to late-August, and it's an incredible sight. Who will you bring and how will you spend the day? Did you remember to bring a hat? Time for some sun!

📍 Around 3, Shimokiyoto, Kiyose-shi

🚆 Kiyose Station and bus

📞 042-492-5111

🕐 Check website

🚫 –

- Participate in the photo contest.
- Locally picked fresh produce is available for purchase.

A striking hike for Adventurer's Day

Mitake

🚶 Mount Mitake

August 30 is Adventurer's Day, so what better time for an adventure? Mount Mitake's popularity rivals that of Mount Takao. Why? The plethora of myths and urban legends that surround this rumored spiritual spot. Ayahiro Falls, where a god of exorcism was enshrined, is particularly otherworldly. The only shrine in Tokyo dedicated to mountain gods, Musashi Mitake Shrine sits at the peak of Mount Mitake. Get to the top by cableway for an easy climb back down. This mountain is fun for people of all ages, every season, all year round.

📍 Mount Mitake, Ome-shi

🚌 Mitake Station and bus
Note: The kanji for Mount Mitake 御岳山 and the kanji for Mitake Station 御嶽駅 are different

📞 0428-78-8121
(Mitake Mountain Railway)

🕐 7:30 am – 6:30 pm

🚫 –

- The Mount Mitake Autumn Leaves Festival sounds like a blast.
- Become a ninja at the Tenku Ninja House.

End the summer with a bang!

Photo by: SPACE SHOWER TV

A summer festival in front of Mount Fuji

Mount Fuji

🚶 Sweet Love Shower

At the end of summer, the music channel Space Shower TV runs this music festival with an extravagant view of Mount Fuji and Lake Yamanaka. Its lineup of artists, emphasizing Japanese rock, make the event more family-friendly than other summer festivals. Activities like hot-air balloon rides and canoeing will get your blood pumping, but the air at the foot of Mount Fuji will cool you back down. Relax and enjoy the music while surrounded by nature.

📍 479-2, Hirano, Yamanakako Village, Minamitsurugun, Yamanashi

🚉 Mount Fuji Station and bus

📞 –

🕐 Please check the official website

🚫 –

- Held annually from end of August to beginning of September.
- Listen to a concert from a canoe!? Why not?

There's nothing like drinking outdoors

Enjoy unlimited food and drinks at one of Tokyo's largest beer gardens

Shinanomachi

✕ Forest Beer Garden

A favorite annual event, the Forest Beer Garden takes place only in the summertime inside the Meiji Shrine's Outer Gardens. Conveniently located near the Shinanomachi Station, this tranquil oasis of green, with a waterfall to boot, is set right in the heart of the city and is the perfect place for visitors to unwind and socialize. Quench your thirst with a beer or cocktail and go all out with their all-you-can-eat-and-drink BBQ (¥4,200 per person for men and ¥3,900 per person for women for two hours).

📍 Meiji-Jingu Gaien Niko Niko Park, 14-13, Kasumigaokamachi, Shinjuku-ku

🚃 Shinanomachi Station

📞 03-5411-3715

🕐 Check website

🚫 Throughout 2020 for the Olympics; in inclement weather

- Packed during the weekends and holidays, so reservations are recommended.
- Watch the Jingu Gaien Fireworks Festival from here in August.

Get in line for a picture!

© Machiko Hasegawa Art Museum

The art museum of the artist behind Sazae-san

Sakurashinmachi

𓀠 Machiko Hasegawa Art Museum

Sazae-san is a popular Japanese four-panel comic that was adapted into an animated series. This privately owned museum exhibits artwork collected by its creator, Machiko Hasegawa, and her sister. There are also areas dedicated to *Sazae-san*, including a corner of original comic manuscripts and animated footage, dioramas and miniatures of the Sazae family home, as well as a gift shop full of original merchandise. The bronze statues on the road from the closest station, Sazae-san Street, and other photo ops are waiting for you.

📍 1-30-6, Shinsakuramachi, Setagaya-ku

🚃 Sakurashinmachi Station

📞 03-3701-8766

🕐 10:00 am – 5:30 pm

🚫 Mondays (open if holiday, closed next business day), during exhibition preparation, New Year's holidays

• Pose with the characters on the wall.
• Give in to the impulse to buy some *Sazae-san washi* tape.

The place
to meet
Doraemon

© Fujiko-Pro

September 3 is Doraemon's birthday

Noborito

🚶 Fujiko F. Fujio Museum

In Kawasaki, Kanagawa, is a museum brimming with the wonders of Fujiko F. Fujio's creations (reservations required). Here, you can be a part of popular manga character Doraemon's gang and pose with the famous Anywhere Door. You can even mimic Nobita's napping pose on top of the cement pipes. The museum is full of exciting exhibitions such as original manga manuscripts and a replica of Fujiko F. Fujio's studio. Don't you wish you had an Anywhere Door to take you straight there?

📍 2-8-1, Nagao, Tama-ku, Kawasaki-shi, Kanagawa

🚃 Noborito Station and bus

📞 0570-055-245

🕐 10:00 am – 6:00 pm

🚫 Tuesdays, New Year's holidays

- Pick up some limited merchandise at the museum shop.
- Take a pic with the What-If Phone Box.

A metropolitan oasis, right here!

A rooftop garden inspired by Monet's water lilies

Ikebukuro

Seibu Ikebukuro Roof Garden

A place to catch a breath of fresh air in the concrete jungle. It's hard to believe this beautifully relaxing space is on the ninth floor of a department store in Ikebukuro. The water lily garden is inspired by Monet's paintings, and greenery flourishes all over the walls. The food court brings you cuisine from around the world for fast dining. A beer garden event is held during summer, so hurry and make your reservations—it's time to kick back with your friends.

📍 1-28-1, Minami-Ikebukuro, Toshima-ku

🚃 Ikebukuro Station

📞 03-3981-0111

🕐 Oct. – Apr.: 10:00 am – 8:00 pm
Note: Operating times are subject to seasonal changes

🚫 Irregular

- Get a taste of every season in the water lily garden.
- The food menus also change each season.

Let's cool down under the trees

Seek respite in the woods from the last hot gasp of summer

Harajuku

🚶 Yoyogi Park

It's early autumn, but it's still an oven out there. Air conditioning is nice, but sometimes you need something more natural, so pick up a cool drink and head to Yoyogi Park. It's right next to JR Harajuku Station, and getting there's a breeze. The cool shade of the trees and the fountain plaza is ready and welcoming. If it does happen to get chilly, you can head to the plaza for some sun. This is a rare place in the city where you can enjoy the blue skies and the feel of the sun on your skin.

📍	2, Jinnan, Yoyogikamizonocho, Shibuya-ku
🚃	Harajuku Station
📞	03-3469-6081
🕐	24 hours
🚫	Service center is subject to operating times

- Head out near sunset to cool down by the trees and fountain.
- Get some exercise with the rental bicycles.

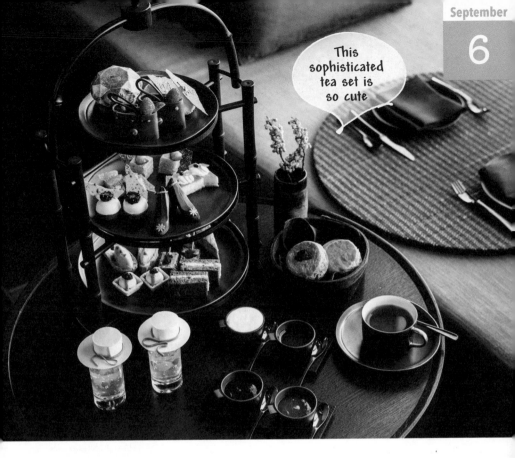

This sophisticated tea set is so cute

An ebony-chic afternoon tea

Otemachi

✗ Aman Tokyo

The number nine is pronounced "ku" and six is pronounced "ro"; put the two together and you get "kuro," or "black" in Japanese. So on September 6, head to the thirty-third floor for some unorthodox charcoal-inspired afternoon tea at The Lounge by Aman. From the seasonal decor to the charcoal-infused bread and sandwiches, to ingredients used in the food and desserts (such as black olives) everything is based on the color black. Even the ink-colored chocolates are so chic you'll want to applaud. The Lounge is popular, so make a reservation!

📍 The Otemachi Tower, 1-5-6 Otemachi, Chiyoda-ku

🚇 Otemachi Station

📞 03-5224-3339 (restaurant reservation line)

🕐 Check website

🚫 –

- Thank you, world, for freshly baked scones!
- The open atrium is so stylish.

Everything
feels special
here

Photo by: STAR BAR GINZA

You'll want to dress up for this

Ginza-itchome

✗ Star Bar Ginza

Tonight, it's time for some of the real deal in Ginza-itchome. The owner and bartender of Star Bar Ginza is the former International Bar Association World Champion. Say cheers with a martini, and treat yourself to a classy, relaxing time. Everything about this bar is luxurious, from the decor to the careful lighting, the fragrance on the hand towels, the ultra-clear ice in the drinks... The welcoming, top-of-the-line service is elegant but not fussy.

📍 B1, 1-5-13, Ginza, Chuo-ku

🚃 Ginza-itchome Station

📞 03-3535-8005

🕐 5:00 pm – 12:00 am

🚫 First Monday of the month

• The seasonal fruit cocktails are a must-try.
• Also try the cheese shaped into rosettes, Tête de Moine.

Pick your own in-season produce

Pick five types of autumn grapes in Setagaya

Kaminoge

🚶 Kimura Grape Garden

Fruit picking is always fun, whatever your age, and this time of year is grape season. There's nothing like eating succulent fruit straight off the vine, and this experience can be yours in Setagaya, Tokyo (pay by the pound for what you pick). From the large, sweet Fujiminori grapes to the popular Shine Muscat, it's peak season for the five types of grapes available. You can also enjoy local produce at the farmer's kitchen on garden grounds.

📍 2-20-16, Noge, Setagaya-ku

🚉 Kaminoge Station and bus

📞 –

🕐 Please check the official website

🚫 –

- You can also dig bamboo shoots, as well as pick vegetables in summer.
- The handmade pizza workshop is bound to be a hit with the kids.

An un"fur"gettable experience!

Let these furry friends give you a pick-me-up

September

9

Machida

🚶 Machida Squirrel Garden

How do you feel about a happy weekend spent feeding squirrels in a squirrel wonderland? In this garden, over two hundred squirrels roam about freely (entry fee applies). If you give them even a glimpse of sunflower seeds, they will surround you. Their big, round eyes and adorable movements will have you clutching your heart. Some of the friendlier squirrels will even climb you! Running around Tokyo is fun, but it'll tire you out, so get some "Awws" in your life to recharge!

📍 733-1, Kanaimachi, Machida-shi

🚃 Machida Station and bus

📞 042-734-1001

🕐 10:00 am – 4:00 pm (Sundays and holidays between Apr.–Sept.: 10:00 am – 5:00 pm)

🚫 Tuesdays (open if holiday, closed next business day); first Tuesday-Friday of June, Sept., and Dec.; New Year's holidays

• Three different types of squirrels have the run of the gardens.
• You can also pet rabbits or guinea pigs.

Just browsing makes you want to pack your bags

A stationery store for world travelers

Nakameguro

🎁 Traveler's Factory

This is a stationery store run by the makers of the popular Traveler's Notebook. Aside from notebooks, the store is filled with tools to make "every day feel like a journey," as well as items to customize those tools. There are leather products, stationery sets, stamps, and even water bottles. From time to time, the store collaborates with other stores or vehicle companies both from Japan and elsewhere. Look for the perfect tools to enrich the journey of life.

📍 3-13-10, Kamimeguro, Meguro-ku

🚇 Nakameguro Station

📞 03-6412-7830

🕐 12:00 pm – 8:00 pm

🚫 Tuesdays

- The Traveler's Notebook is approx. ¥4,320.
- This is the perfect place to find a little gift for someone special.

A festival of camping and movies and the beach

Shuzenji

🚶 Mujinto Cinema Camp

Mujinto means "deserted island," a term sure to excite the adventurous. No deserted island is quite so fun and fulfilling as this, though. Camp by the sound of the ocean, the whispers of the woods, and the light of the stars... Watch a movie under the night sky, and wake up to a posh breakfast buffet. They call it a DIY Cinema Camp Festival, where the campers create the space together for a heart-warming experience (tickets start from ¥10,000). Festival locations change each year.

📍	Changes yearly
🚆	–
📞	–
🕐	Please check the official website
🚫	–

- There are activities like barbecues and kayaking aplenty.
- You can rent tents and sleeping bags at the venue.

What is happening on earth and in the universe right now?!

Telecom Center

🚶 Miraikan

On September 12, Day of the Universe, come find out more about Earth and space at Miraikan (literally "future pavilion"). In the atrium space is Geo-Cosmos, a twenty-foot display of Earth. Pretend you're looking down from outer space, and take in the view. Later, gasp at the powerful films in the high-precision 3-D planetarium Dome Theater. The robot and android workshops will have you exclaiming "Wow!" non-stop.

📍 2-3-6, Aomi, Koto-ku

🚃 Telecom Center Station

📞 03-3570-9151

🕐 10:00 am – 5:00 pm

🚫 Tuesdays (open if holiday),
New Year's holidays

- There are many high-tech activities to participate in.
- Take part in the iPS cell observation experimental workshops.

The entertainment museum of space

Suidobashi

🚶 TeNQ Space Museum

Experience a journey to outer space in the facilities of TeNQ. In the massive, thirty-six-foot-diameter Theater Sora, images of the universe are projected under your feet. The close encounter gives you a sense of floating through space. Take a photograph with the very realistic, slightly scary sculptures of aliens. Limited exhibitions are hosted about three times a year, and collaborations with niche cultures and new films also take place (regular admission ¥1,800).

📍 Tokyo Dome City Yellow Bldg. 6th Fl. 1-3-61 Koraku, Bunkyo-ku

🚆 Suidobashi Station

📞 03-3814-0109

🕐 11:00 am – 9:00 pm
Note: Opens from 10:00 am on weekends, holidays, and other specified days

🚫 –

• Feel the universe with projection mapping.
• Bring home star-shaped accessories and space food as souvenirs.

A café, bookstore, and gallery

大の本

You're sure to find what you're looking for here

Kagurazaka

Kamome Books

Feeling studious during back-to-school season, but can't find the right book? Why not try this bookstore? You'll love that their selection ranges from the new to the old. Some shelves are categorized according to unique themes such as "listen to that little voice," or magazine headline features (think "family," "Tokyo," "fairy tales"). Follow the "bread crumbs" lovingly left by bookstore staff, and nothing you stumble across will be by chance.

📍 123, Yaraicho, Shinjuku-ku

🚉 Kagurazaka Station

📞 03-5228-5490

🕐 11:00 am – 9:00 pm

🚫 Wednesdays (open if national holiday)

- The small gallery-like display is full of fun.
- Kyoto's famous Weekenders Coffee is available here.

September

15

Ditch the digital for old-school vinyl

Chill out with a drink in a record store

Shimokitazawa

🎁 City Country City

You don't get more Shimokitazawa-cool than this second-hand record store/café/bar. The owner has brought back every record from around the world himself, and they're available for a quick listen if you ask. After a leisurely look around, why not try their authentic, handmade pasta, and top off your day with their hot milk with a dash of rum (¥500).

📍 4th Fl. 2-12-13, Kitazawa, Setagaya-ku

🚉 Shimokitazawa Station

📞 03-3410-6080

🕐 12:00 pm – 1:00 am
Weekends and holidays:
11:00 am – 1:00 am

🚫 Wednesdays

- The owner is actually famous singer-songwriter Keiichi Sokabe.
- The store's original buttons make a perfect souvenir.

> I wonder if Grandma would like this?

A box of Edo-style wagashi *happiness for your elders*

Ginza

✿ Ginza Kikunoya

It's almost Respect for the Aged Day. Let's go to this traditional Edo-style *wagashi* (Japanese sweets) shop, established in 1890, and find something to bring back for Grandma or Grandpa. Look for *Fukiyose*, a *wagashi* treasure box filled to the brim with goodies like Japanese cookies, colorful sugar candies, and *wasanbon* (fine-grained Japanese sugar candy). Owls are nestled in the center of "Forever" as a symbol of longevity and wisdom, making this a perfect gift for the important elders in your life.

📍 B1, 5-8-8, Ginza, Chuo-ku

🚇 Ginza Station

📞 03-3571-4095

🕐 11:00 am – 8:00 pm

🚫 –

- Customize a candy plaque called *Unpei* (literally "flat cloud") for gift-giving.
- Try the popular Macadamia Nut Fried *Manju* (sweet dumpling with filling).

As a token of appreciation...

Note: Image for illustrative purposes only

Give a priceless experience instead of a present

Hibiya

🏨 Imperial Hotel Tokyo

Traveling with your elders? Why not skip a physical gift for Respect for the Aged Day and give a lavish hotel experience? The Imperial Hotel started as a state guest house in 1890, and has been beloved since, due to the luxurious space and its impeccable service. For dinner, may we suggest Imperial Hotel's legendary Chaliapin Steak, which is made from the tenderest cut of rump meat? And Marilyn Monroe fans will love knowing she once stayed at this hotel.

📍 1-1-1, Uchisaiwaicho, Chiyoda-ku

🚇 Hibiya Station

📞 03-3504-1111 (Representative)

🕐 Check-in 2:00 pm
   Check-out 12:00 pm

🚫 –

- There are 16 restaurants, bars, and lounges to choose from.
- The premium tower floor delivers a night view of Tokyo.

Feel the life force of Earth!

A flower shop dedicated to Kenyan roses

Hiroo

🎁 Afrika Rose

Parked on a corner of Hiroo Shopping Street is a flower shop that carries only roses from Kenya. Grown in highlands where the changes in temperature are harsh and dramatic, these flowers are powerful and beautiful, vibrant with vivid colors and unique patterns. A single rose from Afrika Rose is enough of a statement, but a bouquet is sure to make an impact on your special someone. It's said that marriage proposals involving these flowers have had a one hundred percent success rate. Ready to pop the question? Pick a rose up for good luck!

📍 5-18-8, Hiroo, Shibuya-ku

🚃 Hiroo Station

📞 03-6450-3339

🕐 11:00 am – 8:00 pm

🚫 Thursdays of July and August, New Year's holidays

- These gorgeous roses are fair trade.
- Check out the flower arrangement lessons.

One of Tokyo's few outlet shopping malls

Aomi

⚏ VenusFort

When the weather's cooled down a little, you might feel an urge to update your wardrobe for the new season. The most famous shopping mall of the Daiba area, VenusFort, is known for its Sky Feature ceiling, which changes with time. Paired with the European-style interior, this mall is a fantasy world of its own. There are around 170 shops, with the first floor being dedicated to family-friendly shopping, the second to the latest fashion trends, and on the third floor, outlet shops you seldom find in Tokyo. Everyone's bound to find something they want here.

📍 1-3-15, Aomi, Koto-ku

🚃 Aomi Station

📞 03-3599-0700

🕐 Shops: 11:00 am – 9:00 pm
Restaurants: 11:00 am – 11:00 pm
Note: May differ between shops and seasons

🚫 Irregular

- The outdoor space is full of fun events.
- In winter, the mall is turned into an illuminated wonderland.

Be moved by the never-ending sea of buildings

© TOKYO-SKYTREE

Climb the world's tallest tower on *Sky Day*

Tokyo Skytree

📷 TOKYO SKYTREE®

September 20 is Sky Day. Climb the tallest tower in the world and gaze down at the incredible vista like a bird in flight (a combo ticket for Tembo Deck and Tembo Galleria is available). When the skies are clear, the view of the Kanto area spans from the nearby Sensoji Temple all the way to Mount Fuji. At night, the glittering cityscape against the sparkling sky is out of this world. At Sky Restaurant 634 (musashi) on Tembo Deck Floor 345, be blown away by fusion Japanese cuisine prepared with a combination of French techniques and Edo-Tokyo concepts.

📍 1-1-2, Oshiage, Sumida-ku

🚉 Tokyo Skytree Station

📞 0570-55-0634

🕐 8:00 am – 10:00 pm

🚫 –

- Win a lottery to see the new year sunrise or the Sumida River fireworks from Skytree.
- The Fast Skytree Ticket for International Visitors lets you skip the line.

Make sure you visit this legendary bar

Photo by: Yuki Nakajima

Times and people change, but not this bar

Asakusa

🍴 Kamiya Bar

This place is legendary. Established in 1880, Asakusa's Kamiya Bar was the first bar built in Japan. Ask for the famous *Denki Bran*, literally "electric brandy," created by the original owner of Kamiya Bar (¥270). A brandy-based liquor infused with herbs, its alcohol percentage is thirty percent. At Kamiya, the tradition is to chase it down with beer. When you feel like getting buzzed on something strong, Kamiya is the place to go.

📍 1-1-1, Asakusa, Taito-ku

🚃 Asakusa Station

📞 03-3841-5400

🕐 11:30 am – 10:00 pm

🚫 Tuesdays

- The beer comes directly from the Asahi beer factory.
- The stew, made with premium konbu stock, is a must-try.

A toy you can live in!

See the artwork you can stay the night in

Musashisakai

🚶 Reversible Destiny Lofts Mitaka

Built in memory of Helen Keller, the colorful, woodblock-like appearance of Reversible Destiny Lofts Mitaka are sure to catch your eye. Enter and be welcomed into an extraordinary space that excites all your senses with its fourteen ultrachromatic colors, spherical rooms, bumpy floors, and other features. And yes, you can stay the night in this work of art (three night minimum). The creators of the space, Shusuke Arakawa and Madeline Gins, said it themselves: "This piece is only complete when someone is living in it."

📍 2-2-8, Osawa, Mitaka-shi

🚃 Musashisakai Station and bus

📞 0422-26-4966

🕐 Check website for visit and lease times

🚫 –

• Every corner is a photo opportunity.
• The rooms are available for long-term lease.

Experience a night at the museum for real

The night museum to drop into on your way back

Tokyo

🚶 Mitsubishi Ichigokan Museum

There's something thrilling about the phrase "a night at the museum," isn't there? As fall rolls in, indoor activities become a little more enticing. How about some leisurely time in a retro museum? Restored to its former 19th-century glory, this brick building in front of Tokyo Station draws your attention. Open until 9:00 pm on Fridays, it is romantically illuminated at night. Instead of heading straight back to your hotel after a day of sightseeing, meander a little off-course and explore (ticket prices depend on the exhibition).

• Exhibition tie-in menus are available at Café 1894.

📍 2-6-2, Marunouchi, Chiyoda-ku

🚃 Tokyo Station

📞 03-5777-8600 (call center)

🕐 10:00 am – 6:00 pm
Note: Excluding holidays, Fridays, second Wednesdays of the month, and weekdays of the last exhibition week are open until 9:00 pm

🚫 Mondays (open if holiday or last week of exhibition), New Year's holidays

Dumplings you could stare at forever

Photo by: sjr_38

The dumplings that taste as good as they look

Shinjuku-sanchome

✖ Oiwake Dango

A generous daub of red bean paste on snow-white dumplings is quite an unforgettable sight. Here at this long-established specialty store, the *dango*, or rice dumplings, taste as good as they look. The traditional flavors are always a classic, but the Ginger or Sweet Soy Sauce dumplings are popular too. There's a Japanese café in the back where you can sit and savor them. Pictured above are Sweet Soy Sauce, Red Bean Paste, and Matcha Paste (all three for ¥761). They are sold by the skewer, so don't be afraid to swing by and get one to go.

📍 3-1-22, Shinjuku, Shinjuku-ku

🚃 Shinjuku-sanchome Station

📞 03-3351-0101

🕐 11:00 am – 6:30 pm
Weekends and holidays:
11:00 am – 7:30 pm
Takeout window:
10:00 am – 8:30 pm

🚫 New Year's Day

- This is a great place to relax in the middle of Shinjuku.
- Try the summer-special shaved ice if you get a chance.

The crystalline dessert found in Omotesando

Omotesando

Mikan Club

If it weren't for the *kinako* and black sugar syrup around it, you'd probably never think this was edible. This beautiful, glass-like dessert The Angel's Tear Set is as clear as the tears after which it is named (limited quantities available). It's so bouncy and slippery, it runs away from your attempts to eat it. The dessert is a *mizu manju* (Japanese jelly cake) made from healthy, low-calorie seaweed. The Sweet Soy Sauce Dumpling Set that you grill yourself is exciting as well.

- 1st Fl. 4-15-2, Jingumae, Shibuya-ku
- Omotesando Station
- –
- 12:00 pm – 5:30 pm
  Weekends and holidays: 11:00 am – 5:30 pm
- Mondays (open if holiday)

- The Japanese tea in the dessert sets is delicious.
- The atmosphere of the renovated traditional Japanese home is magical.

They look like tomes of magic...

This number of books (twenty-four thousand) is quite the spectacle

Sengoku

🚶 Toyo Bunko Museum

This glorious wall of books is called Morrison's Stacks, a collection of twenty-four thousand books purchased by the founder in 1917. At Toyo Bunko, there are over one million important texts, including five national treasures and seven government-designated important cultural artefacts (entry fee ¥900). Feel as if you're lost in a labyrinth with the clever light design of the exhibition as you travel through the history of books. Photographs are permitted everywhere on the premises, so find your perfect shot.

📍 2-28-21, Honkomagome, Bunkyo-ku

🚇 Sengoku Station

📞 03-3942-0280

🕐 10:00 am – 7:00 pm

🚫 Tuesdays (open if holiday, closed next business day), New Year's holidays, other irregular days

- After your tour, take a break at the Orient Café.
- Try the book-shaped Bunko Lunch.

Let's read into the night

Photo by: koyama

Get lost in a world of books

Shinsen

🚶 Mori No Tosyo Shitsu

The name means Forest Reading Room, and this library-cum-bar is indeed a forest of books. This welcoming space is hidden away from the chaos in Shibuya. Once you become a member (membership fee is ¥10,800 per year), cover fees are waived, and you can leave your favorite book with their collection along with a message of your choice, along with other enticing perks for bibliophiles. The midnight closing time is a perk of its own, too.

📍 3rd Fl. 5-3, Maruyamacho, Shibuya-ku

🚆 Shinsen Station

📞 03-6455-0629

🕐 12:00 pm – 5:00 pm
6:00 pm – 12:00 am
Weekends and days before holidays: 12:00 pm – 12:00 am

🚫 Irregular

• Get some self-care with a glass of wine and a book.
• Try the menu that recreates dishes from books.

You'll almost forget this is Tokyo!

Photo by: anygoldman

Mother Nature's embrace just twenty minutes from Shibuya

Todoroki

🚶 Todoroki Valley

A little over half a mile long, Todoroki Valley is the only valley in the twenty-three wards of Tokyo. Near the entrance, descend from the steps by the bright red Golf Bridge, and an untamed dome of green stretches over you. The bustle of the city you heard just moments earlier vanishes as you continue down the riverside walkway. In fall, the foliage blushes a deep shade of red, and you are graced with another taste of Japanese nature. The valley is full of sites to visit like Japanese gardens, ancient tunnel tombs, and the Fudo falls, so have fun exploring.

📍 2-37 to 2-38, 1-22, Todoroki, Setagaya-ku

🚉 Todoroki Station

📞 03-3704-4972

🕐 –

🚫 –

- Rest at the Japanese sweet shop Setsugetsuka, at the base of Fudo Temple.
- Bento meal boxes are available at the small plaza near the top.

A magical tunnel!

A corridor of green for ¥150

Higashi-Mukojima

📷 Mukojima-Hyakkaen Gardens

Hagi, or bush clover, are in full bloom around this time of year. At the magical Bush Clover Tunnel in Mukojima-Hyakkaen Gardens, free your body and soul from stress. The tunnel of green is speckled with lovely small pink flowers. And guess what? The entry fee is only ¥150. The garden is two hundred years old, and full of flowers and plants that bloom year round. A brisk walk around the premises is enough to revitalize anyone. You don't need to get out of Tokyo to refresh your spirit.

📍 3, Higashi-Mukojima, Sumida-ku

🚃 Higashi-Mukojima Station

📞 03-3611-8705

🕐 9:00 am – 5:00 pm

🚫 Dec. 29 – Jan. 3

- The sunbeams scattering through the tunnel are so photo worthy.
- May is another great time to visit for the new greens of spring.

© The National Museum of Western Art

The world heritage art museum

Ueno

🚶 The National Museum of Western Art

This is the only UNESCO World Heritage Site in all of Tokyo. This art museum was designed by one of the pioneers of modern architecture, Le Corbusier. From its open atrium to spiral hallways, the building itself is a marvel. Paintings, sculptures, block prints, even craftwork—this museum has a wide collection of over six thousand pieces of work spanning across media, styles, and eras.

📍 7-7, Ueno Park, Taito-ku

🚃 Ueno Station

📞 03-5777-8600 (call center)

🕐 9:30 am – 5:30 pm
Fridays and Saturdays:
9:30 am – 8:00 pm (permanent and planned exhibitions)

🚫 Mondays (open on holidays closed next business day), New Year's holidays

- Take a commemorative photo in front of the Rodin sculpture outside.
- The permanent exhibition is free on the 2nd and 4th Thursdays of the month.

On October 1, fall in love with a Japanese garden

Korakuen

🚶 Koishikawa Korakuen

October 1 is Tokyo Citizen's Day, when all city-managed parks and museums are free to enter. Koishikawa Korakuen is one of those gardens, so if you've never been, make the best of this chance. The moon bridge made full by its reflection on the water, a recreation of Arashiyama's Oi River, and other surprising historical sights are waiting to be discovered. If you like what you see, come back again during cherry blossom and fall foliage season.

📍 1-6-6, Koraku, Bunkyo-ku

🚇 Korakuen Station

📞 03-3811-3015

🕘 9:00 am – 5:00 pm

🚫 Dec. 29 – Jan. 1

- The drooping cherry blossoms during cherry season are simply stunning.
- In fall, the deep red autumn foliage is gorgeous.

Winter in advance!

The first Japanese ski resort to open each season

Gotemba

🚶 Snow Town Yeti

Located at the second station on the south side of Mount Fuji, this ski resort is well known for being the first to open each year. If you're itching to hit the hills, skip the wait and head to Yeti. Yeti has all-nighter (3:30 pm – 8:00 am) days scheduled each year for those of you who can't get enough. There are also gentle toboggan slopes and snow playgrounds for family-friendly fun.

📍 2428 Aza Fujiwara, Suyama, Susono-shi, Shizuoka

🚌 Gotemba Station

📞 055-998-0636

🕐 Check website

🚫 –

- Not driving? Get there easily by train and bus.
- Weekends and holidays are packed full of events for kids.

That soothing feel
of clay between
your fingers!

Throw a few at this metropolitan studio

Aoyama-itchome

🚶 Pottery School Yukobo

Art is fun to appreciate, and even more fun to create. At Pottery School Yukobo, you can make your own works of art with their one-day workshops. Throw down some clay and turn the potter's wheel, or pick a ceramic piece for painting and decorating. Aside from the Hand-Shaping course for bowls or cups, there's also the flexible "I Wanna Make This" Lesson, which lets you pick what you want to make, including large plates, pasta bowls, soup bowls, or anything else of your choice.

📍 5th Fl. Mihashi Bldg. 1-3-3,
Kita-Aoyama, Minato-ku

🚉 Aoyama-itchome Station

📞 03-6447-0234

🕐 Depends on the class

🚫 Mondays

- I Wanna Make This Lesson: Plates is a two-hour course (¥5,400).
- Silversmith and leathercraft workshops are also available.

It's like we're in Vietnam!

Host the trendiest SEA party here

Shinjuku

✕ Sanagi

Highly recommended for a fun night out. Under an overpass in Shinjuku is a mystical space rich with South East Asian atmosphere. Reminiscent of Hoi An, the host of lanterns suspended above is the definition of Instagrammable. Inside, the theatrical food court serves rotisserie and satay, dim sum and noodles, *oden* and sushi rolls, vegetable dishes, and drinks from four night-market-style food stalls. By the way, October 4 is Girls' Night Out Day.

📍 Under the Highway 20 overpass, 3-35-6, Shinjuku, Shinjuku-ku

🚇 Shinjuku Station

📞 03-5357-7074

🕐 11:00 am – 11:30 pm

🚫 Irregular

- Even the washrooms are cute, so go check it out.
- There's a standing bar, gallery, and even a performance stage.

Parfait in every flavor!

End your day with sweet dreams at this parfaiteria

Shibuya

✗ Parfaiteria beL

In Hokkaido, people don't wrap up a night of drinks with something hot and savory like ramen—they have fruit-filled parfaits! And popular night-time parfait specialty shop, Parfaiteria PaL has finally opened a sister shop in Tokyo. Topped with seasonal fruit, spices, and herbs, the sophisticated flavors of these parfaits are yours to savor until late into the night. Get one to recharge at the end of your day, or stop by with your friends for a late-night get-together.

📍 3rd Fl. 1-7-10, Dogenzaka, Shibuya-ku

🚉 Shibuya Station

📞 03-6427-8538

🕐 5:00 pm – 12:00 am
Fridays, Saturdays and days before holidays: 5:00 pm – 2:00 am

🚫 –

- Alcoholic beverages are available.
- Attractively hand-drawn menus with helpful explanations.

ホワイトチョコと
抹茶のマフィン
¥230

Come here if you're on the hunt for new bread discoveries

秋茄子チリコンカン
まみの少ないチリコンカンをベー
スに、ジューシーなナスとクルミが
アクセント！
¥300

コアントローロークリーム
カスタードクリームにオレンジの香り
とまろやかな甘さのリキュール（コアン
トロー）が入った大人のクリームパン！
¥200

カフェオレあんぱん
カフェオレ味のあんことホイップ
クリームが中に入っています。
¥200

チョコ
中にチョコチップ
そのままでザクザ
¥2

The bread lover's favorite event of the year

Ikejiri-Ohashi

✕ La Fête du Pain Setagaya

Do you like bread? If your answer is yes, don't miss this event. In early October, over 140 accomplished bread makers and boulangeries from around Japan gather here for the biggest bread event of the year. Just how many types of melon bread can be found in one place!? When you stumble upon a creation you've never seen before, you'll barely be able to contain your excitement. You could spend all day enjoying these doughy delights.

📍 2-4-5, Ikejiri, Setagaya-ku

🚃 Ikejiri-Ohashi Station

📞 –

🕐 Please check the official website

🚫 –

- There are multiple unique bread-making workshops to participate in.
- Pick up some festival souvenir merchandise.

Healthy food for cold weather

© YES TOKYO

For bodies that need a little boost

Nakameguro

🎁 Yes Tokyo

October 7 is Diet Awareness Day. If you're looking for healthier alternatives to cold-weather comfort food, try this place. In Tokyo, veggie portions and options in restaurants leave many of us unsatisfied, but maybe the superjuices from Yes Tokyo, simply called Cold Press Juice, can help. Full of nutrition and fiber from legumes and fruits, these juices will give your body a boost. Find the right juice for you from the twenty types available on their menu.

📍 1-3-11, Kamimeguro, Meguro-ku

🚃 Nakameguro Station

📞 03-3760-4717

🕐 10:00 am – 8:00 pm
Weekends and holidays:
10:00 am – 7:00 pm

🚫 –

• Try their protein smoothie or popular acai bowls.
• Check out the joint yoga studio.

The air in the mountains just feels better

Photo by: momo/PIXTA

What you get when you put "Tokyo" and "hiking" together

Takaosanguchi

🚶 Mount Takao

If you're feeling a craving for exercise, get ready to sweat on a hike at Mount Takao (*Takaosan*). There are nine different trails to the top, including the Suspension Bridge Course and Biwa Falls Course, and there's plenty to see along the way. Take a refreshing walk through the woods just as the leaves are about to change colors. When you get to the top, you'll feel as good as new both inside and out. Don't forget to stop for the famous *Mitsufuku Dango*. The freshly grilled dumplings are so chewy and yummy, you'll feel recharged instantly.

📍 Takaomachi, Hachioji-shi

🚆 Takaosanguchi Station

📞 042-664-7872 (Tokyo Takao Natural Park Management Center)

🕐 Check website for cableway operation times

🚫 –

- For beginner hikers, we recommend Trail No. 1.
- Cableways and elevators are available, so take it easy if you need.

It's surprisingly hard to go straight!

Photo by: Keisei/PIXTA

The swan boats are hard to resist

Kichijoji

🚶 Inokashira Park

Kichijoji is one of the most popular residential areas in Tokyo. Famous for its view of cherry blossoms in spring, its fall foliage is just as spectacular. Get away from the chaos of the city and freshen up with a walk around the lake. Enjoy the park however you like—be it appreciating the reflection of the red leaves on the waters as you drift on a swan boat, or getting the warm fuzzies from the cute creatures at Inokashira Park Zoo. Incidentally, October 9 is Take a Walk Day.

📍 1-18-31, Gotenyama, Musashino-shi

🚉 Kichijoji Station

📞 0422-47-6900

🕐 24 hours

🚫 –

• Try the hot dogs from the stand near the entrance.
• Stop for lunch at the in-park café, Pepacafé Forest.

Blow on that before you eat it!

The famous oden you eat with plum miso

Odawara

✗ Odawara Oden Festival

You may have heard of oden, a type of hot pot dish with ingredients you can choose from, but have you heard of Odawara's *oden*? This style is served with the delicacy of the region, plum miso paste, along with everything from fishcakes made by long-established stores to hard-boiled eggs. The festival dedicated to these *oden* happens just as it really starts to get cold outside. Blowing the steam off hot *oden* in Odawara Castle Park feels perfect in the chilly weather.

📍 Ninomaru Plaza, Odawara Castle Park, Odawara-shi, Kanagawa

🚃 Odawara Station

📞 0465-20-0310

🕐 Check website

🚫 –

- Souvenir *oden* are available to take home.
- The plums used in the miso paste are picked locally at Odawara-Soga.

The finger food your fingers can't stop reaching for

Golden snacks for breaks on your Asakusa adventure

Asakusa

✘ Oimoyasan Koushin

This is a chain of sweet potato specialty stores you'll see all over Asakusa, starting with the one operated by a potato wholesaler on Asakusa Denpoin Street. These fried, syrup-covered potato snacks are a traditional Japanese finger food, and the type of potato used changes from season to season. Fry the best potatoes until they're perfectly crisp, then drizzle some secret-recipe syrup on top, and your snack, *daigaku imo*, is complete! Every bite of the sweet, syrup-infused potato is full of irresistible flavor. If you're in Asakusa, it's not to be missed.

📍	1-36-6, Asakusa, Taito-ku
🚇	Asakusa Station
📞	03-3843-3886
🕐	9:00 am – 8:00 pm
🚫	–

- Get them delivered frozen to your doorstep.
- Potato *yokan* (paste-jelly snack) and other desserts are also available.

Hold nothing back tonight!

Get a taste of celebrity life in Tokyo

Shibuya

🚶 Trump Room

A ceiling full of sparkling chandeliers and walls lined with lavish mirrors—this captivating space is positively out of the ordinary. If you want a peek into another type of Tokyo night life, you've come to the right place. This gorgeous event space, which appeared in the movie *Helter-Skelter*, can be rented out for weekend parties, and is also frequently used for fashion-related events and photoshoots. It's fun thinking about all the famous (and infamous) people who have passed through here.

📍 4th and 5th Fl. 1-12-14, Jinnan, Shibuya-ku

🚉 Shibuya Station

📞 03-3770-2325

🕐 Check the official Facebook page for event information

🚫 –

• They say VIPs from around the globe secretly visit this spot.
• Pay attention to the period-style furniture imported from Europe.

Go bold or go home!

The vintage clothing shop like an overturned toy chest

Shibuya

Nude Trump

If you're looking for some daring pieces to set yourself apart from the crowd at the party, this vintage shop in Shibuya is the right place. Sequinned dresses, wild animal print accessories— this small room is bursting at the seams with glittering items reminiscent of the '80s NYC party scene. With a selection like this, it's no wonder stylists and models frequent Nude Trump.

📍 3rd Fl. 1-12-14, Jinnan, Shibuya-ku

🚉 Shibuya Station

📞 03-3770-2325

🕐 1:00 pm – 9:00 pm

🚫 –

- Pick up something fun for Halloween.
- The women's-only store Rosy-Baroque is on the 6th floor.

Time is passing slowly, somehow

Photo by: Kominato Railway

A retro-adorable stop-over escapade

Goi

📷 Kominato Railway

October 14 is Railway Day, so all aboard the retro-cute local railway on the Boso Peninsula. First, look at how cute the carriages are! As you thumpity-thump your way down the tracks, gaze out of the windows and see familiar places like Kazusaokubo Station of *Totoro* fame, popular film location Kazusatsurumai Station, and other beautiful places you'll want to make stopovers for. Drop by the hot springs at Yoro-Keikoku Station to enhance your journey even further.

📍 2-1-11, Goichuonishi, Ichihara-shi, Chiba (Start)

🚌 Goi Station

📞 0436-21-6771 (9:00 am – 5:30 pm)

🕐 Check website

🚫 –

- We also recommend coming during cherry blossom and canola blossom season.
- You can also rent bicycles at Yoro-Keikoku Station.

Even in fall, there's still something for flower fans

Photo by: momo/PIXTA

Sway on the trains, ride the Ferris wheel, feel the cosmos

Kasai-Rinkai Park

📷 Kasai-Rinkai Park

Cosmos flowers are synonymous with fall in Japan, and the best way to see them is to ride the Keiyo Line to a park with a patchwork field of pink and yellow cosmos blossoms. Get on the Diamond and Flowers Ferris Wheel in the park, and be dazzled by the view of the cosmos fields and blue waters of Tokyo Bay. (They say this Ferris wheel was the model for a famous scene in the manga *Honey and Clover*.) After getting your fill of fall scenery, head to the Kasai-Rinkai Aquarium next door. Looks like today will be an exciting day!

📍 6-2, Rinkaicho, Edokawa-ku

🚃 Kasai-Rinkai Park Station

📞 03-5696-1331

🕐 24 hours

🚫 The service center is subject to operating days/hours

- Have lunch at Blue Marine inside the park.
- The main attraction of the aquarium is the Tuna Swarm.

Fresh produce from the source, in Aoyama

Omotesando

⚙ Farmers' Market @ UNU

This farmers' market is open every weekend at the plaza in front of United Nations University. Farmers and greengrocers from around the country gather to sell their finest fare under these tents. In Japan, you don't get many chances to speak directly with the people who produce your food. Aside from vegetables, processed products such as malt and jam, DIY tools, and miscellaneous merchandise are also available. Why not pick up some fresh ingredients from trustworthy sources and cook everything yourself this weekend?

📍 5-53-70, Jingumae, Shibuya-ku

🚆 Omotesando Station

📞 03-5459-4934

🕐 10:00 am – 4:00 pm (may change due to weather conditions)

🚫 Opens every Saturday and Sunday

• Try attending the bread festivals and other events, too.
• Check the official website for a list of vendors.

Made in Japan

Learn traditional Japanese dyeing from local artisans

Kuramae

🎁 MAITO Kuramae

A charming atelier and textile shop located in Kuramae, MAITO Kuramae has garnered a reputation for beautiful, uniquely Japanese products—painstakingly handmade using the traditional Kusakizome dyeing technique. Native plants like sakura blossoms and Yaku cedar are used to color natural fabrics without the use of harsh chemicals. From knits and shirts to bags and other goods, shoppers have plenty of options. You can also sign up for a workshop to get hands-on experience!

📍 1st Fl. 4-14, Kuramae, Taito-ku

🚃 Kuramae Station

📞 03-3863-1128

🕐 11:30 am – 6:30 pm

🚫 Mondays

• Stores also located in Akihabara and Okachimachi.
• Reservations required in advance for workshops.

Play ping-pong and drink at the same bar

Kuramae

🚶 Ribayon

Located right by the Sumida River, you can get a full view of Tokyo Skytree from Ribayon's large windows. Climb up to the fourth floor, take your shoes off, enter and you'll be greeted by a ping-pong table nestled in a chic, modern bar. Yes, you can play ping-pong here, and for free! Get buzzed on their selection of over one hundred types of whiskey and liquor, and also get some exercise. Who doesn't love some co-ed sport?

📍 4th Fl. 2-15-5, Kuramae, Taito-ku

🚃 Kuramae Station

📞 03-5820-8210

🕐 6:00 pm – 1:30 am
Weekends and holidays:
5:00 pm – 1:30 am

🚫 –

- Relax in the at-home feel of the lounge.
- Try the Pork and Lettuce *Shabu-Shabu* if you're hungry.

Beer and ping-pong—a perfect match

How about some ping-pong after this?

Shibuya

🚶 Shibuya Ping-Pong Club

After getting that first drink after work, you might be interested in having a second here, in Shibuya Ping-Pong Club. This stylish ping-pong club is just a minute's walk away from Shibuya Station. Shoe rentals are free. While you're waiting for your own ping-pong showdown, enjoy your favorite drink. The club is open until 5:00 am, so if you're a night owl this is the place for you! Just keep an eye on the train timetable if you're relying on public transport.

📍	1-14-14, Shibuya, Shibuya-ku
🚌	Shibuya Station
📞	–
🕐	10:00 am – 5:30 am
🚫	–

- Wonder what's the beer of the month?
- Switch to darts or bowling once you've had enough ping-pong.

> Fall fireworks are spectacular in the cold air

The Enoshima fireworks festival

Katase-Enoshima

📷 Enoshima Fireworks Festival

Fireworks festivals are generally more of a summer tradition, but the fireworks launched in fall to winter weather look especially vibrant in the clear, crisp air. From Katase Beach, Enoshima peeks out from the left, and over three thousand fireworks are launched, including No. 20-size fireworks, which bloom into flowers of fire over nineteen hundred feet wide. Their brilliant reflection on the seawater will leave you speechless. Explore Enoshima during the day, and enjoy the fireworks at night. Not too shabby.

📍 West side of Katase Nishihama Beach, Fujisawa-shi, Kanagawa

🚆 Katase-Enoshima Station

📞 0466-22-4141 (Fujisawa Tourism Center)

🕐 Check website

🚫 –

- The festival takes place in mid-October every year.
- The sunset from the west side of Katase Beach is simply wonderful.

Italian sodas with homemade syrup and the finest sandwiches

Shibuya

Tokyo Kenkyo

Tokyo Kenkyo sits between Shibuya and Daikanyama, a quaint and humble café. In this warm space lined with tasteful furniture, you can sit down with decorated sodas and delicious sandwiches. The syrup used in the Italian sodas is homemade with kiwi, pomegranate, and even persimmons and other seasonal fruits. They pair amazingly with the generous sandwiches, stuffed full of toppings like fried pork or mashed potatoes.

- 7-9, Nanpeidaicho, Shibuya-ku
- Shibuya Station
- 03-6416-4751
- 8:00 am - 8:00 pm
- Mondays

- There are usually at least eight types of syrup available.
- The favorite, Ultra-Thick Fried Pork Cutlet Sandwich, is recommended.

© Disney

Halloween is a great time to visit Tokyo Disney Resorts

Maihama

🚶 Disney Halloween

Tokyo Disney Resorts have a strict rule against dressing up and cosplay, but it does not apply during Halloween season. You can dress like the characters from head to toe, and inside the park, you'll see other guests doing the same. The decorations and colors will get you pumped for Halloween. The performances and parades are also event-limited, and they're a joy to watch. Even if you're a little shy, just one cosplay item in your get-up should double the fun.

📍	1-1, Maihama, Urayasu-shi, Chiba
🚉	Maihama Station
📞	0570-00-8632 (Information Center)
🕐	Check website
🚫	–

- The Halloween-themed foods are highly Instagrammable.
- Check the official website for more about the event and cosplay rules.

Step into a picture-book world

Enter a fairy-tale world, including magical wall art

Kichijoji

✗ Hattifnatt

Kichijoji is teeming with trendy, quirky cafés. This one makes you feel like you've lost your way in a magical picture book. The art is by a picture-book illustrator, and the walls are covered in drawings of children and animals. Stay for a cup of tea and abandon yourself to a land of imagination. The Indulgent Baked Ganache (¥540) doesn't hold back on the ganache, and is a must-try. They pride themselves on only whipping the cream after they've received your order.

📍 2-22-1, Kichijojiminamicho, Musashino-shi

🚇 Kichijoji Station

📞 0422-26-6773

🕐 11:30 am – 10:00 pm
Fridays and Saturdays:
11:30 am – 11:00 pm

🚫 Irregular

- There are alcoholic drinks on the menu, so night visits are also recommended.
- Visit the shop next door.

Coffee and a book— heaven!

Loiter in this stylish Tsutaya

Daikanyama

🎁 Tsutaya Books, Daikanyama

This is the posh bookstore you have to stop by if you're in Daikanyama. Just one peek inside, and you'll see the overwhelming selection of books and magazines stacked throughout the store. Other than books, there are areas dedicated to rare movies, stationery from around the world, and music that most Tsutaya shops don't carry. It's a world of arts and media coming together. Grab a Starbucks coffee and spend a few hours inside.

📍 17-5, Sarugakucho, Shibuya-ku

🚇 Daikanyama Station

📞 03-3770-2525

🕐 7:00 am – 2:00 am

🚫 –

- Check out the international magazine selection at Magazine Street.
- On the second-floor lounge, do some reading with a glass of wine.

The garden looks like framed art

Daikanyama

📷 Old Asakura House

While you're in Daikanyama, make sure you stop by the Old Asakura House as well. It is an outstanding example of Taisho period architecture, and was declared an Important Cultural Property by the Japanese government in 2004. The surrounding gardens, decorated with tasteful objects like stone lanterns, offers lovely views of azaleas in spring and red maples in autumn. During fall foliage season, popular foliage sites will be crowded, but here, you can enjoy the scenery at your leisure.

📍 29-20, Sarugakucho, Shibuya-ku

🚃 Daikanyama Station

📞 03-3476-1021

🕐 10:00 am – 6:00 pm
November to February:
10:00 am – 4:30 pm

🚫 Mondays (open if holiday, closed next business day), New Year's holidays

- Entry fee is a bargain at ¥100.
- The unchanged century-old painted screens add to the charm.

It's all here! Ramen that impresses even ramen-iacs!

Komazawa-daigaku

✗ Tokyo Ramen Show

Today is the day to stuff yourself with ramen outdoors! One of the biggest events of its kind, around thirty-six types of ramen make an appearance throughout the event. Some ramen featured previously include Katsuryu, a rich sea urchin ramen from Ibaraki, and Yamako Project, a premium salt-based ramen from Osaka with a rich sea bream and blue king crab broth. Here you can try original ramen you won't find anywhere else.

📍 1-1, Komazawa Park, Setagaya-ku

🚃 Komazawa-daigaku Station

📞 –

🕐 Check website

🚫 –

- Go with a group and share the joy.
- They're open on weekdays, too, so head over any time.

Take care of yourself and our planet, too

An organic festival for the environmentally conscious

Harajuku

♊ Yoyogi Craft Fair

This is the fall edition of a seasonal arts and crafts event run by Earth Garden, an organization dedicated to producing comfortable, balanced lifestyles that respect the earth and the environment. In the venue, Yoyogi Park, around two hundred tents are filled with unique handmade crafts. Organically made merchandise like clothing and other useful items are available for your browsing pleasure. On the outdoor stage, there are live performances, and there's plenty of food to be had too. These festivities guarantee a day of fun that's gentle on the planet.

📍 2-3, Jinnan, Shibuya-ku

🚉 Harajuku Station

📞 03-5468-3282

🕐 Check website

🚫 –

• Attend all the workshops you can!
• The flea market for outdoor sporting goods is a treasure cove.

It's time to collect yourself

A church to help you collect yourself

Ochanomizu

🚶 Holy Resurrection Cathedral

Some people think of this cathedral, an Important Cultural Property designed by the father of modern Japanese architecture, Josiah Conder, as the symbol of Ochanomizu. Its magnificent exterior is more than enough to take in, but the tour inside is also highly recommended (entry fee ¥300). Behind the doors is a beautiful world of stained glass and icons, purifying your soul. If you're feeling overwhelmed, this is a great place to collect yourself.

📍 4-1-3, Kandasurugadai, Chiyoda-ku

🚇 Ochanomizu Station

📞 03-3295-6879

🕐 1:30 pm – 3:30 pm
Apr.–Sept. 1:00 pm – 4:00 pm

🚫 Always open for prayer (may be closed for weddings or funerals)

- See for yourself what mass is like in this cathedral.
- While you're in the area, also hit up the Illusion Art Museum nearby.

A Turkish mosque right here in Tokyo

Often called the most beautiful mosque in Asia

Yoyogi-Uehara

🚶 Tokyo Camii & Turkish Culture Center

October 29 is Turkey's Republic Day, and how better to celebrate than going on a mini-trip to "Turkey"? Open the geometrically patterned doors and head to the second floor, where this gorgeous mosque, which many consider the most beautiful in Asia, is waiting for you. If you plan on entering the mosque, please make sure you pay close attention to and respect their instructions.

📍 1-19, Oyamacho, Shibuya-ku

🚆 Yoyogi-Uehara Station

📞 03-5790-0760

🕐 Visiting hours 10:00 am – 6:00 pm

🚫 –

- At 2:30 pm on weekends, Japanese guided tours are available.
- Attend the Turkish cuisine cooking classes.

Tokyo by bike is pretty great!

It's the Tour de Japon! A bike tour around Tokyo

Ariake

🚶 Bike Tokyo

You'll see a whole new side of Tokyo if you travel by bike, and this thirty-one-mile bike trail that will take you from some of Tokyo's most well-known sights, all the way to secret hole-in-the-wall spots. This cycling event takes place in chilly October to November, and working up a sweat has never felt so good. There's nothing like a self-powered excursion to help make you feel a little more like Tokyo is your city.

📍	3-8-35, Ariake, Koto-ku
🚃	Ariake Station
📞	03-3354-2300 (WizSpo!! office)
🕐	Check website
🚫	–

- Electric bicycles are available for rent, so you can take it easy.
- A guide cyclist leads the way, so you're in safe hands.

Pumpkin!
Pumpkin!
Pumpkin!

For Halloween, a pumpkin dessert specialty shop

Sangenjaya

✕ Kabocha

Pumpkin lovers, don't pass out when you see this dessert shop, simply named "Pumpkin" in Japanese. You have your Pumpkin Maple Chiffon, Premium Smooth Pumpkin Pudding, Pumpkin Mont Blanc, and Pumpkin Gateau Chocolat. Every single dessert brings out the best of a pumpkin's mellow sweetness. The Halloween-season cookies are perfect for trick-or-treaters. Which one are you gonna choose?

📍 2-38-10, Sangenjaya, Setagaya-ku

🚉 Sangenjaya Station

📞 03-5481-1553

🕐 10:00 am – 8:00 pm

🚫 Irregular

- The icing cookies are just too cute.
- Take home some Pumpkin Toast for breakfast.

Want to tour Tokyo on bike? This is the right place

Sendagi

🚶 Tokyobike Rentals Yanaka

If you find trains stuffy and uncomfortable, and wish you could slip through the crowd and breeze through Tokyo on a bike, this shop is here to grant that wish. Operating out of an eighty-year-old renovated *sake* shop, Yanaka sells and rents Tokyobikes for riding in the city. You can also sit down inside for something to drink. Inside, bike trail maps and recommended course maps are available, too. Start here and you're in for a fulfilling day.

📍 4-2-39, Yanaka, Taito-ku

🚇 Sendagi Station

📞 03-5809-0980

🕐 10:00 am – 7:30 pm

🚫 Second Tuesday of the month (open if holiday)

• Check the website for rental availability.
• Like the bike you rented? You can buy it.

This is the best book village in Japan

The Jimbocho festival for bookworms

Jimbocho

✸ Kanda Old Books Festival

Every book lover in Japan has heard of Jimbocho, "the town of old books." Every year, people from all over the world congregate here for the massive sale event of over a million books. The main attraction is the Blue Sky Old Book Market. Bookshelves and shop fronts envelop the sidewalks of Yasukuni Street, turning it into a Hallway of Books about a third of a mile long. The Exhibition Sale of books handpicked by store owners is also famous. Put up a little fight at the open Charity Auction, and bring something home.

📍 1, Jimbocho, Kanda, Chiyoda-ku

🚇 Jimbocho Station

📞 03-3293-0161

🕐 Check website

🚫 –

- Held every year between late October and early November.
- Jimbocho is also famous for its curry.

Watch pilots strut their stuff

Photo by: morihiro/PIXTA

Amazing aerobatic demonstrations

Inariyama-koen

📷 Japan Air Self-Defense Force Iruma Base

Make room in your schedule for this! Seeing the Japanese Air Force demonstration team Blue Impulse mark the skies beautifully in person is a chance few people get. The standing ovations and cheers keep coming for the bird-like acrobatic flights as the bright blue skies are turned into a backdrop for the show. All this fun, and it won't cost you a cent. The access from central Tokyo is convenient as well, so don't miss out!

📍 Japan Air Self-Defense Force Iruma Base, Sayama-shi, Saitama

🚌 Inariyama-koen Station

📞 04-2953-6131

🕐 Please check the official website

🚫 –

- Take a picture of the heart of smoke.
- The parachuting demonstration is awe-inspiring, too.

Flawless taste, volume, and presentation

Photo by: tsumugi77

Exquisite fried food that practically jumps out of the bowl

Asakusa

✗ Tentake

November 4 is *Karaage* (Japanese deep-fry) Day. A long line forms outside Tentake regardless of the day, but be sure to save room for their Fried Oysters on Rice. Bursting from under the lid are a ton of oysters, shrimp, squid, and scallops. You'll practically inhale the rice with the ultra-rich sweet-and-spicy sauce as your partner in crime. Even though the food is fried it doesn't sit heavily in the stomach. There's no reason not to indulge!

📍 2-4-1, Asakusa, Taito-ku

🚈 Asakusa Station

📞 03-3841-5519

🕐 10:30 am – 5:00 pm
Weekends and holidays:
11:00 am – 6:30 pm

🚫 Mondays (open if holiday, closed next day)

• Who cares if it's daytime? Grab a cold one with the oysters.
• Try the conger eel *Jotendon* (literally "premium tempura on rice").

You can "fish" for this charm!

Fish for happiness with these omikuji!

Musashi-nitta

🚶 Nitta Shrine

This shrine is the origin of *hamaya*, the arrow-shaped protection charm you often see in shrines around New Year's Eve. But they're also a bulls-eye for people looking for love charms. Inside shrine grounds, there's the Love Shrine (said to bring couples happiness if they take a photo together in front of it), a Stone Ping Pong Table, and other curious and fun spots. For single folk looking for romance, we suggest the heart-shaped *ema* and the Lucky Love Charm. By the by, November 5 is Matchmaking Day.

📍 1-21-23, Yaguchi, Ota-ku

🚉 Musashi-nitta Station

📞 03-3758-1397

🕐 9:00 am – 5:00 pm (office)

🚫 –

• The sea bream charm you can fish up is ¥300 a try.
• The original *hamaya*, Arrow Protection Charm, should be of benefit.

There's a secret as to why their right paws are raised...!

Pray for love with fortune cat ema

Asakusa

🚶 Imado Shrine

Now's the perfect time to pray for some matchmaking magic. This shrine is known as the birthplace of the fortune cat. Most fortune cats you see have their left paws up to pray for prosperity and riches, but the cats at Imado Shrine have their right up for people and connections. On shrine grounds, there are even married fortune cats! We recommend you try the Victory of Love Fortune, rumored to sometimes yield "Super Duper Excellent Luck." This shrine is also famous among people looking for marriage.

📍 1-5-22, Imado, Taito-ku

🚉 Asakusa Station

📞 03-3872-2703

🕘 9:00 am – 5:00 pm (office)

🚫 –

• The round *ema* for eternal happiness (¥700) is popular, too.
• Some say if you set a fortune cat as your screen wallpaper, your wishes will come true.

Make a design request!

The incredible Mentai Motsu Hot Pot is so good, it should almost be illegal!

Shibuya

✗ Hakata Motsuraku Shibuya

As the new season starts, hot pot tastes extra good. *Mentaiko* (pollock roe from Fukuoka) and *motsu* (offal) are Kyushu specialties, and both are widely loved. This hot pot restaurant combines the two into a menu of your dreams. Plump, juicy *motsu* and spicy *mentaiko* are a match made in heaven. Book your reservation early, and the staff will arrange the *mentaiko* in the shape of a heart for a special celebration. Also, November 7 is *Motsu* Day.

📍 B1, 26-3, Udagawacho, Shibuya-ku

🚋 Shibuya Station

📞 03-5728-7599

🕐 5:00 pm – 12:00 am
Fridays, Saturdays, days before holidays: 5:00 pm – 2:00 am
Sundays, holidays:
4:00 pm – 11:00 pm

🚫 –

• Snap a pic quick before the *mentaiko* melts!
• Opening and closing times may change during summer.

Candles made simple and cute

Photo by: Candle Studio Tokyo Main School

Handmade candles to light your long autumn nights

Omotesando

🚶 Candle Studio Tokyo

To make your fall nights even more romantic, make some lovely candles of your own. Here, you can make donut-shaped dessert candles, classic aromatic candles, botanical candles with seasonal plants, and more. Don't worry, it's as easy as putting decorations on a cake. And the aromatic wax sachets don't need to be burned to fill your room with their scent; they can be enjoyed as is.

📍 4-25-12 Minami-Aoyama, Minato-ku

🚆 Omotesando Station

📞 03-5656-1927

🕙 10:00 am – 9:00 pm (subject to change)

🚫 New Year's holidays

- Come for one-time lessons, or the full certification course.
- Wax decoration lessons are also available.

Infinite variations!

Hunt for one-of-a-kind Converse sneakers

Meiji-Jingumae <Harajuku>

White Atelier by Converse

November 9 is Nice Shoes Day, so it's a good excuse to go and create your own Converse sneakers. At this store, you can find limited original All Stars designed by artists or pick from over sixty standard designs to print onto your shoes. Finish them off with original laces and charms for an even more personal touch.

📍 B1, 1st Fl. 6-16-5, Jingumae, Shibuya-ku

🚇 Meiji-Jingumae <Harajuku> Station

📞 03-5778-4170

🕚 11:00 am – 8:00 pm

🚫 Irregular

- You can even print just one initial on each shoe to make your pair.
- Don't forget to check the store-limited Converses.

Make yourself a one-of-a-kind shirt

Make your custom T-shirt under 5 minutes

Shibuya

🎁 Arton

Make a truly one-of-a-kind T-shirt at Arton. Bring in your own design, and within five minutes, you'll have your shirt! (One shirt starts from ¥2,800.) It doesn't stop at T-shirts, though. Tote bags, hoodies, even leggings! The more you print, the less it costs, so you might like to do a group order with friends.

📍 4th Fl. 17-1, Udagawacho, Shibuya-ku

🚇 Shibuya Station

📞 050-5539-6625

🕐 12:00 pm - 9:00 pm

🚫 –

• Make matching shirts for a friend's birthday.
• A unique pair of shirts for your parents' anniversary sounds fun, too.

Flowers and tea make a good match

Take a breather before heading home

Omotesando

✕ Aoyama Flower Market Tea House

This is the nicest-smelling café in all of Omotesando. Every visible corner of the café is filled with botanical blessings, but the best view in the house is from the counter seats, where you can see the atrium garden. The dish to ask for is the vegetable Garden Bowl. Desserts like Rose Jelly and Flower Parfait are also worth keeping on your to-eat list. The days are getting chilly, and you'll want to stay warm with some fresh herb tea.

📍 5-1-2, Minami-Aoyama, Minato-ku

🚊 Omotesando Station

📞 03-3400-0887

🕐 11:00 am – 8:00 pm
Sundays and holidays:
11:00 am – 7:00 pm

🚫 New Year's holidays

- Go in for a fresh mojito on the way home.
- In winter, try the Hot Mojito.

Photo by: samenosuke/PIXTA

A great place for some quiet fun

Nagatoro

📷 Nagatoro

Nagatoro refers to not one particular spot, but to a whole area in Saitama. You can get to this scenic place by Chichibu Railway. Along the Arakawa River, walls of rock line the waters for a third of a mile, adding to the aesthetic. In fall, the beautiful foliage ramps up the elegance. Go on a boat ride downriver, as the view from there is also extraordinary. In winter, some boats are even equipped with heated *kotatsu* seats! During festival times, the Tsukinoishi Momiji Park is illuminated at night.

📍 Nagatorocho, Chichibugun, Saitama

🚉 Nagatoro Station

📞 0494-66-0307 (Nagatoro Tourism Information Center)

🕐 Check website

🚫 –

- The natural-ice shaved ice at Asami Reizo is a must-have.
- Nagatoro is also known for its whitewater rafting.

There's something special about fall festivals, right?

Turn the heat up with a festival for prosperity!

Shinjuku-sanchome

🚶 Hanazono Shrine

On November's Day of the Rooster, the Tori no Ichi festival is celebrated. Merchants come to procure extravagantly decorated rakes as a prosperity charm, but simply browsing and eating from all the food stalls is plenty of fun. The most famous attraction of all is the Freak Show and its jaw-dropping performances. Among the entertainers are a human flamethrower, a singing severed head, and a woman who eats live chickens. Photography and recordings are strictly prohibited, so what happens inside, stays inside…

📍 5-17-3, Shinjuku, Shinjuku-ku

🚊 Shinjuku-sanchome Station

📞 03-3209-5265

🕐 Check website

🚫 –

- The shrine is said to bring luck for those looking for new connections.
- It also brings luck for artists and artisans.

Winter is coming

And I'll huff, and I'll puff, and I'll gulp them all down!

Gotokuji

✗ Yakiimo Specialty Store Fuji

The steam rises as the lid comes off, revealing sweet potatoes resting on a bed of hot rocks. There's no sight quite like it, and it means winter has truly come. Here's a rare example of a *yakiimo* (Japanese hot-stone-roasted sweet potato) specialty shop in Tokyo. You can try roast potatoes made with unusual varieties such as the "carrot potato" and "Halloween sweet," carefully selected and delivered from all around Japan. For winter, we recommend the sweet and sticky *beni haruka* potato.

📍 1-7-11, Gotokuji, Setagaya-ku

🚆 Gotokuji Station

📞 03-6413-7215

🕐 10:00 am – 7:00 pm

🚫 –

- The roast taro looks so good on camera.
- You can choose between small, medium, and large potatoes.

Did you know about this historical figure's connection to Sumida?

© Forward Stroke

Learn about the Japanese artist who took the world by storm

Ryogoku

⚘ The Sumida Hokusai Museum

This Hokusai-filled museum will steal your attention with its mirror-like exterior before you even get inside. In the unique slitted spaces, exhibitions about the world-famous *ukiyo-e* master take place. In the permanent exhibition (entry fee ¥400), be wowed by not only the *ukiyo-e* works of art, but the century-old giant ema that was restored with the newest technology, interactive touchscreens, and 4K high-definition presentations. Also visit the nearby Edo-Tokyo Museum and Sumo Museum while you're in the area.

📍 2-7-2, Kamezawa, Sumida-ku

🚉 Ryogoku Station

📞 03-5777-8600 (call center)

🕐 9:30 am – 5:30 pm

🚫 Mondays (open if holiday, closed next day), New Year's holidays

- *Ukiyo-e* merchandise are more stylish than you'd think.
- There is a library of *ukiyo-e* books inside.

Photo by: KAWAII MONSTER CAFE

Another dimension of "Harajuku Kawaii!" from the source

Meiji-Jingumae <Harajuku>

Kawaii Monster Cafe

This one is popular with the tourists! Designed by the father of "Harajuku Kawaii," Sebastian Masuda, this café is practically a theme park. The cake-shaped merry-go-round features a unicorn sucking on a baby bottle, just to give you an idea. The menu won't let you down, either. The rainbow-colored pasta and hyperchromatic cakes are a visual shock, but a good one.

- 4th Fl. 4-31-10, Jingumae, Shibuya-ku
- Meiji-Jingumae <Harajuku> Station
- 03-5413-5142
- 11:30 am – 4:30 pm
  6:00 pm – 10:30 pm
  Sundays and holidays:
  11:00 am – 8:00 pm
- –

- Come at night, too!
- There's something deep about the classy cabaret feel.

Stunning autumn color worth coming back for every year

Take a photo in the center of this golden scene

Aoyama-itchome

📷 Jingu Gaien's Ginkgo Trees

This is the golden face of Tokyo that only shows itself during fall. You'll want to get up early to get a few snaps of the yellow carpet of fallen leaves before it's disturbed by the bustle of the day. An icon of Tokyo fall scenery, it's beautiful in daytime, but even more romantic at night, when the rows of trees are illuminated by street lamps. The Ginkgo Festival takes place in late November, and out come all the delicious food stalls. Bring your gloves and scarf, and go for a slow walk with the important people in your life.

📍 2, Kasumigaokacho, Shinjuku-ku

🚇 Aoyama-itchome Station

📞 03-3401-0312

🕐 24 hours

🚫 –

- Famous shops from Tokyo set up booths.
- The ginkgo at Showa Kinen Park are gorgeous as well.

The time-travel destination one hour away

Photo by: Kawagoe Location Service

The 8th, 18th, and 28th are all Kawagoe Kimono Day, so put one on and head out

Kawagoe

🚶 Kawagoe Kurazukuri Town

"Little Edo" Kawagoe is just an hour away from Shinjuku. The tasteful and rustic *kurazukuri* (buildings built in the style of warehouses called *kura*) townscape are a match for traditional Japanese clothing. When you get there, the first thing to do is rent a kimono for the day. Then head to the old shopping district to try the enormous *Osatsu* chips, and the *Nekomanma* (a rice dish with bonito flakes) rice balls. Buy some cheap snacks for souvenirs at the traditional Japanese penny candy shop, and enjoy the time-travel adventure into a retro Japan.

📍	Kawagoe-shi, Saitama
🚉	Kawagoe Station
📞	Depends on store
🕐	Depends on store
🚫	Depends on store

- Sit down in a retro café on Taisho Romance Street.
- Stop by the Kawagoe Hot Springs for a day trip.

A store full of sweet elegance

Kawaii *from around the globe*

Omotesando

🎁 Miss Faline

Stroll along the row of color-changing ginkgo trees, all the way to Omotesando. A pink wall and giant neon signs will come into sight. This is a select shop opened by one of Harajuku's original icons, Babymary. Treat yourself to *kawaii* (cute) fashion from around the world. Collaboration T-shirts with illustrator Antoine Kruk and other original pieces are popular as well. Feel pretty in this pink space!

📍	3-6-26, Kita-Aoyama, Minato-ku
🚇	Omotesando Station
📞	03-5766-2558
🕐	12:00 pm – 9:00 pm
🚫	Irregular

- Even the shutters you'll see when the shops close are adorable.
- Falinetokyo in Harajuku is the sister store.

A must for watch enthusiasts!

Gift yourself an authentic Japanese custom watch

Kichijoji

🎁 Maker's Watch Knot

A small watch brand that started in Kichijoji, Knot has since expanded to multiple locations. Knot's beautiful, uniquely crafted watches are manufactured and assembled domestically, and the manner in which their merchandise is laid out—the watches and their components are displayed separately out in the open—gives customers the opportunity to mix and match styles, creating watches of their own design. Treat yourself to a custom watch today!

📍 2-33-8, Honcho, La Ruelle Kichijoji 1F, Kichijoji, Musashino-shi

🚉 Kichijoji Station

📞 0422-27-6360

🕐 11:00 am – 7:00 pm

🚫 Irregular holidays

- Choose from over twenty thousand styles.
- Shops are also located in Omotesando, Marunouchi, and Yokohama Motomachi.

November 21 is Fried Chicken Day!

Chicken + Waffles + Maple Syrup = The Best Decision

Shibuya

✗ Moja in the House

This high-impact specialty, Waffle Chicken, is juicy fried chicken you drench in maple syrup before digging in. The salty batter and sweetness of maple deliver consecutive blows to your taste buds, while the mellow waffle lends some gentle padding to soften the attack. The more you chew, the more you fall captive to the chicken's finger-licking goodness. The spacious restaurant has over one hundred twenty seats, accommodating your needs for sofa seating with friends, or counter seats for a one-person meal.

📍 2nd Fl. 1-11-1, Shibuya, Shibuya-ku

🚇 Shibuya Station

📞 03-6418-8144

🕐 11:00 am – 11:00 pm

🚫 New Year's holidays

- The filling steak is super tasty.
- The sodas are mixed with house syrup, too.

Unbelievable value for the money

Classy conveyer-belt sushi for Good Partners Day

Tokyo

Nemuro-Hanamaru

This is the Marunouchi Kitte branch. If you want slightly upgraded conveyor-belt sushi, this is the right place. The restaurant swears upon the good name of their hometown Nemuro, famous for seafood, to bring their guests fresh, mouth-watering toppings. The secret to Hanamaru's success are the fair prices for toppings you can't find at most comparable sushi restaurants, such as Red King Crab Belly (¥345), or Salmon Roe in Soy Sauce (¥345). The generous servings of roe roll off the rice like pearls—you might well be overwhelmed!

Address	5th Fl. 2-7-2, Marunouchi, Chiyoda-ku
Station	Tokyo Station
Phone	03-6269-9026
Hours	11:00 am - 11:00 pm Sundays and holidays: 11:00 am - 10:00 pm
Closed	–

- In winter, the Cod Milt and Fatty Mackerel are excellent choices.
- The Blue King Crab Miso Soup (¥345) is value for money.

Look for the pup and the leaves!

Photo by: SIN/PIXTA

A park with the most curious Takamori Saigo statue

Ueno

📷 Ueno Onshi Park

More commonly known as Ueno Park, this is where you'll find a statue of Takamori Saigo, one of the most famous and influential samurai of the Edo and Meiji periods, with...his dog! It's also fantastic for enjoying the warm colors of fall. You'll want to add a shot of the vibrant foliage woven around the pagoda to your album. Not to mention, the in-park Starbucks Coffee is open, making it a perfect spot to refuel after an autumn stroll. The park is frequently host to seasonal events such as Taiwan Festival or Nepal Festival, so it's worth coming back often.

📍	3 Ikenohata/Ueno Park, Taito-ku
🚃	Ueno Station
📞	03-3828-5644
🕐	5:00 am – 11:00 pm
🚫	–

- Home to The Ueno Royal Museum, The National Museum of Western Art, and more.
- The contrast between Shinobazu Pond (Shinobazu no Ike) and the city skyline is simply gorgeous.

Love the late hours for weekday visits!

Autumn color at Rikugien. Photo by: bxv_obee_s785

The most romantic autumn illumination in Tokyo

Komagome

📷 Rikugien

In fall, the traditional gardens of Rikugien are vibrant with foliage during the day, but there's a whole other world of color to enjoy at night. Rikugien really set the benchmark for illuminated gardens: imagine the rich reds of Japanese maple lit up to look like flames in the darkness. In contrast to the warmth of the leaves, a blue illumination called *Suikoue* creates a breathtaking effect of flowing water on the ground. Stay warm, because you'll want to stay longer to take it all in.

📍 6, Honkomagome, Bunkyo-ku

🚌 Komagome Station

📞 03-3941-2222

🕐 9:00 am – 5:00 pm (9:00 am – 9:00 pm during illuminations)

🚫 –

- Enjoy some *matcha* in the park at Fukiage Tea House.
- The park becomes a winter wonderland after some snow.

These facilities are way too cheap!

Musashi-Koyama

🚶 Musashi-Koyama Hot Springs Shimizuyu

You could easily make a one-day hot spring trip out of visiting this bathhouse located in Shinagawa Ward. There are two types of hot spring that you can soak in. The open-air Golden Hot Spring is rich in minerals, and is said to be great for your skin, while Blackwater Hot Spring is amber-colored spring water from deep under the seabed, a cool couple of million years old. Head in for a full course of cleansing and self-care!

📍 3-9-1, Koyama, Shinagawa-ku

🚉 Musashi-Koyama Station

📞 03-3781-0575

🕐 12:00 pm – 12:00 am
Sundays: 8:00 am – 12:00 am
Holidays: 12:00 pm – 12:00 am

🚫 Mondays (open if holiday)

- Even the cold bath uses hot spring water!
- Try the homemade *onsen tamago* (eggs slow-cooked in hot spring water)!

Enjoy some wall art while you soak

Photo by: ayumi iguchi / @aymgch

A cartoon-cute bathhouse for Nice Bath Day

Shin-Koiwa

🚶 Isshinyu

Tucked away in old-town Tokyo is this artistic bathhouse. On the tiled wall in the women's bath is a mosaic illustration of adorable bears and raccoon dogs happily carrying a *mikoshi* (portable Shinto shrine). The mascot character of bathhouses in the Edogawa Ward, a sumo wrestler shaped like Mount Fuji named Hot Spring Fuji, can also be found in various spots around the place. Put Isshinyu on your Tokyo bathhouse list!

📍 4-9-8, Matsushima, Edogawa-ku

🚇 Shin-Koiwa Station

📞 03-3651-6313

🕐 3:30 pm – 10:30 pm

🚫 Mondays

- Check out the extensive celebrity autograph collection.
- Take a look at Hot Spring Fuji's belly button on the shutters.

This is a dessert!

Surprise them with an artistic dessert

Meiji-Jingumae <Harajuku>

✗ Solomons

For a planned surprise on birthdays or anniversaries, this restaurant is down to help. In particular, the artistic dessert that gets its finishing touches on the table, F.O.Y.T. (Finish On Your Table), will be sure to make the recipient happy. The scrumptious meals and trendy interior offer bang for your buck, so consider Solomons for your girls' nights or private events. Another dish that gets its final, fiery touches at your table, the Flaming Cheese Risotto, is popular as well.

📍 B1, 2-31-20, Jingumae, Shibuya-ku

🚃 Meiji-Jingumae <Harajuku> Station

📞 03-6434-9201

🕐 11:30 am - 2:30 pm
5:30 pm - 10:30 pm
Weekends and holidays:
11:30 am - 2:30 pm
5:00 pm - 11:30 pm

🚫 –

- The menu is full of surprises, like the Glowing Champagne.
- Their limited Christmas multicourse meals are also popular.

November

28

Photo by: Yuta Hayashi @SPICE AVEDA Coppice Kichijoji Branch

Have a breakfast that feels like a trip to France

Shibuya

Viron Shibuya Branch

A line forms outside this bakery before it even opens. Up a little early? Come get the elegant Morning Set (¥1,620). The baguette bread-lovers say "smells like France," and it comes with six jars containing a choice of jam, honey, or chocolate cream. A breakfast as stylish and delicious as this and you'll think you're in Paris. You should also know that November 28 is French Bread Day.

- 2nd Fl. 33-8, Udagawacho, Shibuya-ku
- Shibuya Station
- 03-5458-1776
- 9:00 am - 10:00 pm (Breakfast: 9:00 am - 11:00 am)
- –

- So glad that breakfast is served until 11:00 am.
- The Baguette Rétrodor is a must-take-to-go.

This isn't meat! It's art!

Meat sushi taken to the next level

Roppongi

✕ GyuGyu Nishi-Azabu

Simply good *yakiniku* just won't cut it any more... On Good Meat Day, you'll want something that's a feast for the eyes, too. Dishes such as "The longest premium *gyutan* (ox tongue)" and the gold-foiled Chateaubriand are so extravagant, you can't not snap a few photos. Pandora's Box, Dragon Kalbi with Fireworks, Pot of Yams—fun, gimmicky dishes you won't find elsewhere will make your heart skip a beat.

📍 B1, 1-2-3, Nishi-Azabu, Minato-ku

🚆 Roppongi Station

📞 03-3478-3999

🕐 6:00 pm - 3:00 am
Sundays and holidays:
6:00 pm - 11:00 pm

🚫 –

- The melt-in-your-mouth meat sashimi and sushi are also a must-have.
- You won't be able to stop talking about the sukiyaki-style Tsukimi 3-Second Beef Loin.

Don't mind the others, let your inner child back out in this picture-book café

Shibuya

✕ Bookcafe Days

Whatever your age, the picture books at this dedicated café are sure to appeal. Kick back and relax in a world of stories. You might find the "picture book for life" that you'll want to read to your kids some day. Shiso Rice Omelet, homemade desserts, and other healthy dishes are available. Of course, a trip here with the kids would be a blast. November 30 is Picture Book Day.

📍 1st Fl. Royal Palace, 15-10, Uguisudanicho, Shibuya-ku

🚉 Shibuya Station

📞 03-3461-1554

🕐 12:00 pm – 9:00 pm
Closes at 6:00 pm on Mondays

🚫 New Year's holidays

- Alcoholic beverages are available.
- Guess what? You can rent out the place for a picture-book birthday party.

You won't want to go back to regular seats

PETER LINDBERGH

UNTITLED
116

Photo by: Shinjuku Piccadilly / Shochiku Multiplex Theatres, Ltd.

Enjoy movies on luxurious sofa seats

Shinjuku-sanchome

🚶 Shinjuku Piccadilly

On the first day of the month, or Movies Day, go on a deluxe movie date. At Shinjuku Piccadilly, plush sofa Platinum Seats (¥5,000 per person) are available. Not only are the seats different, even the entrance is separate. An hour before the movie starts, take the exclusive elevator up to the lounge. Enjoy your drinks (included), then move to your viewing seats for the best spot in the house. Sit back and enjoy your movie.

📍 3-15-15, Shinjuku, Shinjuku-ku

🚉 Shinjuku-sanchome Station

📞 03-5367-1144

🕐 Depends on show times

🚫 –

- Frequent guests receive special bonuses.
- The completely private Platinum Room (¥30,000 for two people) is also available.

The light of Enoshima, one of the largest illumination events in the Kanto area

Katase Enoshima

📷 The Jewel of Shonan

If you thought Enoshima was great in summer, wait till you see it in winter. The Jewel of Shonan is the illumination event that takes place all over Enoshima, starting with the Enoshima Sea Candle. The tunnel in Samuel Cocking Garden is covered with over seventy thousand crystal beads, and a walk through feels like seeing the Milky Way. Make some memories this winter at the Jewel of Shonan.

📍 Enoshima, Fujisawa-shi, Kanagawa

🚃 Katase Enoshima Station

📞 0466-24-2715 (The Jewel of Shonan Administration Office Enoshima Railway)

🕐 Check website

🚫 –

- Don't miss the moment of light-up.
- The event continues until Valentine's Day.

色で選ぶ

◆ サンプルを直接レジへお持ちください

Photo by: Ginza/Itoya

Itoya's flagship store will make stationery maniacs tremble

Ginza

✪ Ginza Itoya

Ginza Itoya was established in 1904, and this is its flagship store. The entire building is dedicated to stationery, if you can believe it! The floors are sectioned by themes and purpose like "desk," "letter," or "travel." Around this time of year, you'll want to head straight to the fourth floor for calendars and schedulers to find the perfect journal to keep you company for the new year. Be stunned by the the gradient wall of paper samples on the seventh floor! It's so beautiful, you'll have whipped out your camera before you know it.

📍 2-7-15, Ginza, Chuo-ku

🚆 Ginza Station

📞 03-3561-8311

🕐 10:00 am – 8:00 pm
Sundays and holidays:
10:00 am – 7:00 pm
Café: 10:00 am – 10:00 pm

🚫 New Year's holidays

- Post your letters right away with the in-building post box.
- The veggies in the café are grown on the eleventh floor!

This stationery looks like cosmetics!

The miraculous stationery shop that will make you "your color"

Kuramae

🎁 Inkstand by kakimori

Making a one-of-a-kind, personal color? How cool is that? This "inkstand" allows you to create your own ink by mixing colors from standard inks using an eyedropper. Dip your favorite fountain pen into your newly crafted ink, and leave a mark in your notebook. Why use prepackaged things when you can craft your own? There's something wonderful about making the items crucial to your lifestyle yourself.

📍 1st Fl. 4-20-12, Kuramae, Taito-ku

🚉 Kuramae Station

📞 050-1744-8547

🕐 12:00 pm – 7:00 pm
Weekends and holidays:
11:00 am – 7:00 pm

🚫 Mondays (open if holiday)

- Remember to make a reservation for color mixing.
- To make your own notebook, take the eight-minute walk to the nearby Kakimori.

A great view of Tokyo Tower

A "slope" to stroll down with a loved one on Christmas

Roppongi

📷 # Keyakizaka Illuminations

Which do you prefer? The cool metropolitan shimmer of white and blue LED lights, or the warmth of amber and candlelight-colored ones? The winter illuminations of Roppongi will make you want to spend extra time here with your special someone. As you walk down the lit-up slope, it's like you're in a Christmas episode of your favorite TV show. Make a promise to each other to share a memory like this every year. How does that sound?

📍 6, Roppongi, Minato-ku

🚇 Roppongi Station

📞 03-6406-6000 (Roppongi Hills General Information)

🕐 Check website

🚫 –

- The bridge on Keyakizaka is a great photo opportunity.
- After the walk, how about dinner at Roppongi Hills?

The year is almost over

Who will you share this champagne-gold experience with?

Tokyo

📷 Marunouchi Illuminations

After a day out, wrap things up with some window shopping while enjoying the lit-up streets. During the illumination period, the trees along the streets of Marunouchi Nakadori and Otemachi Nakadori are decorated with around 980,000 original "champagne-gold" LED lights. They are lit up until 11:00 pm, so even the busiest of us can get a chance to enjoy them. Around Christmas, the trees and decorations at Marunouchi Building and New Marunouchi Building are simply gorgeous.

📍 Marunouchi Nakadori, Otemachi Nakadori, around Tokyo Station (planned)

🚉 Tokyo Station

📞 03-5218-5100 (Marunouchi Call Center)

🕐 Check website

🚫 –

- The illumination period is between early November and mid-February.
- Have dinner at Resonance and enjoy the night view.

The creaminess will get ya!

Photo by: takahirokwt

The specialty store for oysters

Gotanda

✗ Tokyo Oyster Bar

December is the time to crave oysters. At this restaurant, you can get a taste of not just Japanese oysters, but those imported from all around the world. Complement your Oyster Platter with wine, beer, or even highballs. After enjoying classics like fried oysters and oyster ajillos, try the unusual Oyster Ice Cream to complete the experience. Tokyo Oyster Bar is the mother to all oyster bars around Japan, and is beloved as an oyster-lover's mecca.

📍 1-11-17, Higashi-Gotanda, Shinagawa-ku

🚃 Gotanda Station

📞 03-3280-3336

🕐 5:00 pm – 10:30 pm

🚫 New Year's holidays

- Taste the difference between Pacific Oysters and Japanese Pacific Oysters.
- Try the wine selected to go specifically with oysters!

You can't even see the rice!

The pork rice bowl that's just too much

Shimbashi

✗ Buta Daigaku

A flower of pork delicately blooming atop a beautiful bowl... Try this sizzling charred pork, dripping with juices, and sweet-and-spicy sauce with a punch of garlic over steaming white rice. All of that will disappear before you know it! There are four sizes to choose from: your standard small, medium and large, or the extra large, which weighs over two pounds (¥1,020)! Add some broth and herbs to the last bit of rice to make a refreshing *ochazuke*.

📍 2-16-1, Shimbashi, Minato-ku

🚇 Shimbashi Station

📞 03-5512-3121

🕐 10:30 am – 9:45 pm
Weekends and holidays:
11:00 am – 3:00 pm
6:30 pm – 8:15 pm

🚫 Irregular; second Sunday of odd months

- A soft-boiled egg is the perfect topping.
- Sprinkle some fried garlic on top to make it even better.

A foot bath on the way home... Oh, yeah!

A foot bath massage café to unwind at

Naka-Okachimachi

🚶 Hogurest

If you're feeling the cold and have some aches and pains to attend to, come to this on-trend foot bath café, Hogurest Total Care Salon + Café. The services start at ¥780 for an hour, one drink included. The Bath Massage service is highly recommended: receive a head, shoulder, and back massage while you soak your feet. When your muscles have relaxed, enjoy a cup of organic herb tea, and you'll feel recharged. A great place to ensure your heart and body are completely rested for the final push before the new year.

📍 3rd Fl. T&T Okachimachi Bldg. 4-8-5, Taito, Taito-ku

🚉 Naka-Okachimachi Station

📞 03-6803-2971

🕐 11:00 am – 10:00 pm

🚫 New Year's holidays

• The café's signature popcorn sounds yummy.
• Professional reflexology and Thai massages are available.

It's cold outside, let's spend a lazy day indoors

Photo by: Ofuro Café Utatane

Relax until nighttime

The Railway Museum

🚶 Ofuro Café Utatane

"I want to relax and chill after the hot springs!" "In fact, I don't want to leave at all!" "Wait, but I want to get something nice to eat." "I just want to read manga all day…" Here, you're free to indulge yourself. Free mud packs are available, and after a long bath, spend the rest of the time however you like. You can even stay the night if you wish. Welcome to paradise for just ¥1,260 yen a day (+¥840 after 2:00 am).

📍 4-179-3, Onaricho, Kita-ku, Saitama-shi, Saitama

🚉 Tetsudo Hakubutsukan Station

📞 048-856-9899

🕐 10:00 am – 9:00 am
Café: 11:00 am – 11:30 pm

🚫 May be closed temporarily for maintenance

- Take a nap or have a get-together in the private rooms.
- Study or work in the workspace area.

A pot full of mushrooms!

Photo by: @shirotan

Shabu-shabu *with a broth made from 30 types of mushrooms*

Roppongi

✗ Shangri-La's Secret

Hojoheitan is a hot pot made with black broth brewed for over eight hours with thirty types of mushrooms imported from around Japan and China. A plethora of mushrooms, including matsutake mushrooms, pearl oyster mushrooms, and mushrooms we've never heard of like the Wild Enoki or Golden Oyster, are all available for *shabu-shabu* along with meat and other veggies. As the dinner goes on, you'll be surprised by the way the black broth gets darker, and the umami grows stronger.

📍 4th Fl. 4-11-11, Roppongi, Minato-ku

🚉 Roppongi Station

📞 03-6804-5095

🕐 11:30 am – 3:00 pm
5:30 pm – 11:30 pm

🚫 –

• The name *Hojoheitan* is borrowed from Chinese.
• They say mushroom extract is good for your skin.

So much grated yam!

Warm your belly with rich tororo hot pot

Roppongi

✕ Tamanoha Guya Nishi-Azabu

A quiet alleyway behind a busy street. When you part the curtains behind the softly lit entrance, you will be welcomed in. What's the best cuisine to warm you in winter? In Japan, it's got to be hot pot. Beef, ginger, intensely spicy—the variety keeps everyone satisfied. The *Tororo* (grated yam) Hot Pot, which you finish by mixing in a generous bowl of *tororo*, is particularly popular. The miso-based broth becomes mellow and rich, and every sip tastes like happiness.

📍 4-2-12, Nishi-Azabu, Minato-ku

🚇 Roppongi Station

📞 03-5464-0908

🕐 5:30 pm – 4:00 am
Weekends and holidays:
5:00 pm – 11:00 pm

🚫 –

• Their signature ox tongue dishes are a must-have.
• The clay pot sea bream and the burdock rice are also delicious.

It's like you're in an American pizza parlor!

For when you want some trendy, yummy pizza

Shibuya

✕ Pizza Slice

From the exterior to the tiles beneath your feet, all the way to the price tags, this New York-style pizza restaurant makes you feel like you've left Japan. "Thin and easy to eat, but still so filling!" is what people say about their pizza. After you get your slice, take a picture with the logo on the tiled floors. On birthdays, the restaurant offers a birthday service including a whole pizza. Check this place out.

📍 1st Fl. 1-3, Sarugakucho, Shibuya-ku

🚉 Shibuya Station

📞 03-5428-5166

🕐 11:30 am – 10:30 pm
Sundays: 11:30 am – 10:00 pm

🚫 Irregular

- You can purchase just one slice, or as many as you want.
- Even the takeout box is so cool.

Smack your lips over melted cheese tonight

Treat yourself to some gooey cheese risotto

Omotesando

✗ Cheese Restaurant Daigomi

Cheese Restaurant Daigomi is a restaurant for cheese lovers, by cheese lovers, with the intention of turning even more people into cheese lovers. In these cheese specialists' hands, anything goes—put it on your food, or have some with drinks. Here you will rediscover the charm of cheese. In particular, The Cheese Maker's Ultimate Stone-Roasted Cheese Risotto is so memorable, you won't be able to stop yourself from filming the goopy cheese as it melts into the bowl.

📍	B1, 6-15-4, Minami-Aoyama, Minato-ku
🚆	Omotesando Station
📞	03-3409-8333
🕐	5:00 pm – 11:30 pm
🚫	Mondays, Sundays

- The one hundred percent Jersey Beef Mozzarella is so good.
- The combination of cheese and gibier (wild game) cuisine is amazing, too.

The live Christmas caroling is lovely

Breathe in the scent of a real fir Christmas tree

Bashamichi

🎁 Yokohama Christmas Market Red Brick Warehouse

This is an authentic recreation of a German Christmas market, and one of its most charming attractions is the line of wood cabins that sell German cuisine and trinkets. The freshly grilled sausages and hot wine taste extra scrumptious in the cold. At the back of the venue is a forty-foot-tall fir Christmas tree, glittering in the night. This is a scene from a picture book. If you're lucky, you may run into Santa Claus!

📍 1-1, Shinko, Naka-ku, Yokohama, Kanagawa

🚃 Bashamichi Station

📞 045-227-2002 (Yokohama Red Brick Warehouse 2nd Warehouse Information)

🕐 Check website

🚫 –

• Who doesn't want a pic with Santa?
• Take home some stollen as a souvenir.

Calm and tranquility just before Christmas

A candle-lit night in a chapel

Omotesando

📷 Aoyama Chapelle Des Anges

When the clock strikes 8:00 pm in winter, the lights in the chapel go out. Close your eyes for just a moment, then open them slowly... A flickering world of candles appears before you. The warm light and silence creates a world of tranquility. The Happy Bell event, where you can write your wishes on a bell and hang them on a Christmas tree, is held in the chapel's garden. A beautiful place like this will relax you and clear your mind.

📍 3-14-23, Minato-ku

🚃 Omotesando Station

📞 03-5411-2722

🕐 Check website

🚫 –

- Illumination period is between November and December.
- A special Christmas mass is held once a year.

Look at those cute eyes

A room filled with hedgehogs, owls, and more

Ikebukuro

🚶 Animal Room Ikemofu

The winter cold can make you feel so lonely... How about cuddling up to some cute animals? This is a space where you can relax and recharge with all sorts of furry friends. We recommend the Petit Animals Room, where you can find bunnies, chinchillas, and hedgehogs. There are also other exotic animals like the fennec fox, kinkajou and prairie dogs. There is also the Owls and Reptiles Room. The fees are approx. ¥1,000 per half an hour, per person, per room.

📍 6th Fl. 1-29-4, Higashi-Ikebukuro, Toshima-ku

🚉 Ikebukuro Station

📞 –

🕐 1:00 pm – 5:30 pm
Weekends and holidays:
11:00 am – 6:00 pm

🚫 –

- Some of the animals are for sale but not others.
- You can have the owl come sit on your arm.

December

18

HARRY

Oh, I just want to take you home!

The prickly idol you want to hold

Roppongi

🚶 Hedgehog Café **HARRY**

Everyone needs a breather sometimes. Some people might be afraid of the prickly hedgehog, but just try giving them a gentle pat (approx. ¥1,400 for thirty minutes). You'd be surprised by how fuzzy they feel in your hands. Despite their bristly looks, they just want to be loved! The way they walk is so unbearably cute, and when your eyes meet, their adorable round eyes will melt you. If you fall in love, you can come back every day.

📍 3rd Fl. 6-7-2, Roppongi, Minato-ku

🚉 Roppongi Station

📞 03-3404-8100

🕐 12:00 pm – 8:00 pm

🚫 –

- Take a picture of a hedgehog in your hands.
- Watch them eat as you give them a snack.

December

19

Beautiful lights that will mesmerize you

Make your own mosaic lamp here

Nippori

🎁 Zakuro House of Lamps

Do you know about Turkish mosaic lamps? These mysterious and exotic-looking lamps can actually be made in two to three hours. At this store, you can create your own standing lamp or a genie lamp with materials imported straight from Turkey. Make a new nightstand lamp for some unusual bedroom decor. Or craft a matching pair with a friend or loved one. Doesn't that sound nice?

📍 3-15-5, Nishi-Nippori, Arakawa-ku

🚉 Nippori Station

📞 03-3822-0610

🕐 11:00 am – 7:00 pm
Weekends: 11:00 am – 8:00 pm

🚫 Irregular (posted on website)

- Apparently this is the only place in Japan where you can make a mosaic lamp.
- The Restaurant Zakuro nearby is said to be amazing.

A spectacular view of Tokyo Station from the rooftop garden

A whimsical white tree to foretell the coming of the Holy Night

Tokyo

📷 White Kitte

Around this time of year, the commercial center in front of Tokyo Station, Kitte, is graced with a Christmas tree decorated to look like it's covered in pure white snow. It is, in fact, a real fir tree, and it's one of the biggest indoor trees in Japan, standing at roughly forty feet. In central Tokyo, white Christmases are rare, but this sight should provide some satisfaction. The event is usually held from late November to late December. (The event is subject to change so check the website first.)

📍 2-7-2, Marunouchi, Chiyoda-ku

🚃 Tokyo Station

📞 03-3216-2811
(10:00 am – 7:00 pm)

🕐 Check website

🚫 –

- A musical illumination is performed once every two hours.
- Pick up some limited Christmas desserts as souvenir.

Doesn't a hot spring date sound nice?

Photo by: meikyozuka

Get in the 164-feet-long foot bath with a loved one

Telecom Center

🚶 Ooedo-Onsen-Monogatari Odaiba

Here we have one of Japan's biggest hot spring theme parks. After reception, proceed to Echigoya to pick up a *yukata* (casual kimono). There is a colorful selection of *yukata* and *obi* (sash) to mix and match. Once you've changed, head to the 164-foot-long foot bath that you and your friends and family can enjoy together. After a good soak, it's time to try your hand at ninja stars and blow darts in the festival games area.

📍	2-6-3, Aomi, Koto-ku
🚌	Telecom Center Station
📞	03-5500-1126
🕐	Morning 11:00 am – next morning 9:00 am
🚫	Closes at 11:00 pm on monthly maintenance days

- The food court is filled with popular restaurants from around Tokyo.
- You can also stay the night, so consider it for your travel plans!

A hole-in-the-wall bathhouse with a Sunday bath special

Ikejiri-Ohashi

Bunka Yokusen

This December, a secret bathhouse—once the setting for a TV drama—will warm up your battered body. Try the Sunday special Medicine Bath. Pomelo, lemon, *tochu* tea, even chocolate; every week a different "medicine" floats in the bath, giving your body and soul the recharge they need. The round Mount Fuji paintings in the bath are also unique.

- 3-6-8, Higashiyama, Meguro-ku
- Ikejiri-Ohashi Station
- 03-3792-4126
- 3:30 pm - 1:00 am
  Sunday 8:00 am - 12:00 pm
  3:30 pm - 1:00 am
- Irregular

- Try the peppermint Cool Cold Bath.
- The Sunday-only morning bath is also recommended.

Spend some time with loved ones here

An early get-together for Christmas Eve

Ebisu

📷 Ebisu Garden Place

The day before Christmas Eve, soak up the atmosphere with Ebisu's winter illuminations (early November to late February, annually). Until early January, a Baccarat chandelier graces the center of the plaza with its crystalline beauty. A thirty-three-foot-tall Christmas tree is also displayed, and photo opportunities are everywhere. Don't forget to check out the limited Christmas market for trinkets and Christmas goodies.

📍 4-20, Ebisu, Shibuya-ku

🚇 Ebisu Station

📞 03-5423-7111

🕐 Check website

🚫 –

• For dinner, find a place with a view of the lights.
• During the event, there are also gospel music performances.

December
24

Christmas Eve right in front of Tokyo Tower

Akabanebashi

✗ Sky Lounge Stellar Garden

The lounge at The Prince Hotel Park Tower Tokyo sits right before Tokyo Tower, and offers an incredible vista of the city. With a view like this, any event is bound to feel special. The cityscape from the windows, the cocktails adorned with edible flowers—everything points to an evening tailored just for you. For those of you getting some alone time this Christmas, get a reservation for the Twilight Premium Plan, which guarantees a view of the tower (limited to five groups of ten people per day).

📍 33rd Fl. 4-8-1, Shibakoen, Minato-ku

🚉 Akabanebashi Station

📞 03-5400-1154

🕐 5:00 pm – 2:00 am
Days before holidays:
3:00 pm – 2:00 am
Weekends and holidays:
3:00 pm – 12:00 am

🚫 –

• The enchanting time between dusk and night is gorgeous.
• Look forward to the seasonal Tokyo Tower illumination.

The magical Christmas Day you've always dreamed of

Maihama

🏨 Tokyo Disney Sea Hotel Miracosta

On Christmas Day, it's time to pack for a night you've always dreamed of at the Miracosta. The rooms are upscale and full of Disney fun. There are Disney characters everywhere you turn, and of course, you must look for the hidden Mickeys. From the windows, you can look out over Disney Sea. It's like you've become a citizen of the land where dreams come true. Just wait till you see the Disney character amenities.

📍 1-13, Maihama, Urayasu-shi, Chiba

🚉 Maihama Station

📞 047-305-2222

🕐 Check-in 3:00 pm
Check-out 12:00 pm

🚫 –

- Hotel guests can enter the park fifteen minutes early.
- Some merchandise is exclusive to hotel guests.

The techniques of Edo are amazing

Handmade Edo brooms so beautiful, you'll want them as decorations

Takaracho

Shirokiya Denbee

Before you know it, it'll be time for spring cleaning. These Edo-style brooms, handmade by a specialty shop that opened in 1830, are lovely enough to hang on your walls. But these things are meant to be used! The makers pride these brooms on being the epitome of well-balanced, light, and easy to use. They can be trimmed at home as well. Use them in the living room, then the bathroom, and as they wear shorter, keep them in the foyer... They say these brooms can last for decades. Now *that's* tradition meeting technique!

📍 1st Fl. 3-9-8, Kyobashi, Chuo-ku

🚃 Takaracho Station

📞 03-3563-1771

🕐 10:00 am – 7:00 pm

🚫 Sundays, holidays

- There are all sizes to meet your needs.
- Brooms with handy, hook-shaped handles are great as well.

好きです この街
とごしぎんざ

グッドマナーでつくろう！日本一住みやすい街
戸越銀座商店街 ✕ Tokyo Good Manners Project

戸越 GINZA

Both heart and tummy are satisfied

Photo by: Togoshi-ginza Shopping Street Association

The shopping street that'll feed you as you walk

Togoshi-Ginza

🎁 Togoshi-ginza Shopping Street

There's no point trying to keep track of all the to-go restaurants among the four hundred stores along this shopping street—there are just too many. There's something for every taste: for example, picture freshly fried *xiao long bao*, and then the steaming *Oden* Croquettes. Next, you'll want something sweet, so how about some creamy soft serve and chewy Arctic Melon Bread made with rice flour... Mmm, so good! Conquer all the food on a gourmet, carefree journey through some of Tokyo's best old-town vibes.

📍	Togoshi, Shinagawa-ku
🚃	Togoshi-Ginza Station
📞	Depends on store
🕐	Depends on store
🚫	Depends on store

- When you've had your fill, take a break at Togoshi Hachiman Shrine.
- Last but not least, knock back a few at Nakatsu Karaage Kei.

December

28

> Get a taste of Tokyo's last days of the year here

Photo by: 7maru / PIXTA

Immerse yourself in the year-end rush in this shopping street

Ueno

🎁 Ameya Yokocho

The Ameya Yokocho Shopping District, more commonly known as Ameyoko, is a shopping street along the JR train tracks between Otemachi Station and Ueno Station. Stores carrying everything from food to clothing are packed tight next to each other. The district formed as a black market after WWII, and now remains one of Tokyo's last historic shopping streets. And it is particularly rowdy at this time of year. Tuna, fish cakes, and other necessities for New Year's feasts can be found for bargain prices. Even just strolling along gets you in the year-end mood.

📍 6-10-7, Ueno, Taito-ku

🚃 Ueno Station

📞 03-3832-5053 (Ameya Yokocho Shopping District)

🕐 Depends on store

🚫 Depends on store

- Ameyoko is also famous for its cheap imported vegetables.
- In the back alleys are famous Southeast Asian dining spots.

© K. Takeshi

What'll the last fireworks of the year be like?

Odaiba-Kaihin Koen

📷 Odaiba Rainbow Fireworks

The year is coming to an end, so on the day before New Year's Eve, head to Odaiba to finish up with a bang. Enjoy the winter skies of Tokyo as they're embellished by beautiful fireworks. The lit-up Rainbow Bridge illuminates Tokyo delightfully, and you won't be able to take your eyes off the spectacle as the fireworks begin in an explosion of light and color. The new year is coming, and soon!

📍 1, Daiba, Minato-ku

🚉 Odaiba-Kaihin Koen Station

📞 03-5564-1202 (Odaiba Rainbow Fireworks Committee)

🕐 Check website

🚫 Weekends and holidays (office)

- About eighteen hundred fireworks are launched in ten minutes.
- Fireworks are launched every Saturday of December (please double-check online for changes).

Don your finest for this classy venue

The restaurant with live music they call the "legendary club"

Tokyo

🚶 Cotton Club

A space with live jazz music and gourmet meals, Cotton Club is a classy place to mingle. The luxury of the legendary club from New York is channeled through the chandeliers and red carpet, creating an elegant and sexy atmosphere for you to kick back in. Dress up for a special occasion, and enjoy a French full-course dinner with refined, live performances as your background music. For an evening befitting the last days of the year, come to Cotton Club.

📍 2nd Fl. 2-7-3, Marunouchi, Chiyoda-ku

🚇 Tokyo Station

📞 03-3215-1555

🕐 5:00 pm – 11:00 pm
Weekends and holidays:
4:00 pm – 10:30 pm

🚫 Irregular (call first)

- Be moved by music by artists from around the world.
- Bring home some original merchandise from the club.

Thank you, Tokyo, for everything!

Cross over to the new year with Toshikoshi Soba

Omotesando

✗ Aoyama Kawakamian

It's the last day of the year. At Kawakamian, you can get toshikoshi soba (buckwheat noodles eaten traditionally on New Year's Eve) until 4:00 am. Pick at the appetizers slowly, hot sake in hand. Before you know it, you'll be tucking into the popular Duck and Green Onion Soba Noodles (approx. ¥1,890). Slurp up this top-of-the-line soba and reflect upon the past year. Then head to the nearby shrine for the first shrine visit of the year while you slowly sober up.

📍	3-14-1, Minami-Aoyama, Minato-ku
🚇	Omotesando Station
📞	03-5411-7171
🕐	11:30 am – 4:30 am
🚫	–

- Dip Soba With Nut Sauce sounds good.
- Try the desserts Soba Dumplings and Crema Catalana.

INDEX

INDEX

March 29 Midtown Blossom
April 2 Canvas Tokyo
April 15 21_21 DESIGN SIGHT
April 25 Jubanukyo
May 9 Melting in the Mouth
May 17 Creative Ochazuke Da Yo Ne
May 20 Midpark Yoga
June 5 The National Art Center, Tokyo
June 6 Shiroikuro
July 20 Hanabusa Tokyo
August 8 New New York Club
September 18 Afrika Rose
November 29 GyuGyu Nishi-Azabu
December 5 Keyakizaka Illuminations
December 11 Shangri-La's Secret
December 12 Tamanoha Guya Nishi-Asabu
December 18 Hedgehog Café HARRY

SHIMOKITAZAWA, MEIDAIMAE, SEIJOGAKUEN-MAE
January 30 Shiro-Hige's Cream Puff Factory
June 28 Cafe Stay Happy
July 22 Shimokita Terrace
September 15 City Country City
November 14 Yakiimo Specialty Store Fuji

JIYUGAOKA, SANGENJAYA, FUTAKOTAMAGAWA
January 8 Today's Special Jiyugaoka
January 9 La Vita
February 9 Claska
February 13 Box & Needle Store
February 20 Snowdome Museum
March 4 Takeno to Ohagi
March 5 The Globe Antiques
March 10 Shaved Ice Café Banpaku
May 3 Kosoan Jiyugaoka
June 13 Waterfront
July 4 "Wa" Kitchen Kanna
September 2 Machiko Hasegawa Art Museum
September 8 Kimura Grape Garden
September 28 Todoroki Valley
October 6 La Fête Du Pain Setagaya
October 26 Tokyo Ramen Show
October 31 Kabocha

TOYOSU, ODAIBA, TOKYO BAY AREA
January 16 Madame Tussauds Tokyo
February 27 Odaiba Kaihin Park
June 2 Shiokaze Park
June 3 Museum of Maritime Science
June 27 teamLab Planets TOKYO
July 23 Wild Magic
July 27 Grand Nikko Tokyo Daiba
September 12 Miraikan
September 19 VenusFort
October 30 Bike Tokyo
December 21 Ooedo-Onsen-Monogatari Odaiba
December 29 Odaiba Rainbow Fireworks

ASAKUSABASHI, RYOGOKU, KINSHICHO, OSHIAGE
January 13 Edo Tokyo Museum
January 20 Kokugikan
January 21 Ryogoku Terrace
February 22 Oshiage Nyanko
July 5 Sumida Coffee
August 6 Asakusa Amezaiku Ame-Shin
August 25 Shake Tree Burger & Bar
September 20 Tokyo Skytree
September 29 Mukojima-Hyakkaen Gardens
November 15 The Sumida Hokusai Museum

ITABASHI, JUJO
February 14 Bonnel Cafe
March 11 Dagashiya Game Museum
June 23 Trampoline Park Trampoland

NAKANO, KICHIJOJI, KOGANEI, KOKUBUNJI
January 4 Asagaya Shinmeigu Shrine
January 19 Karina
March 2 Shooting Bar EA
March 13 Red Heart Store
March 25 Violon
May 15 Dachibin
May 29 Thai Food-stall Restaurant 999
June 1 Edo-Tokyo Open Air Architecture Museum
June 19 Blue Sky Coffee
July 10 Daily Chiko
September 22 Reversible Destiny Lofts Mitaka
October 9 Inokashira Park
October 23 Hattifnatt
November 20 Maker's Watch Knot

TACHIKAWA, HACHIOJI, OME
April 22 Fussa Base Side Street
May 14 Showa Kinen Park
July 9 Ukai Toriyama
August 15 Mount Takao Beermount
August 30 Mount Mitake
October 8 Mount Takao

OTHER PARTS OF TOKYO
January 17 Yomiuri Land
February 2 Mayoterrace
February 4 Sugita Tofu
March 12 Shibamata High Color Yokocho
March 19 Planetarium Starry Cafe
March 26 Tower Hall Funabori
March 28 Chikurin Park
April 20 Fukagawa Winery Tokyo
July 24 Niijima and Shikinejima
July 26 Nippara Limestone Cave
July 29 Lake Okutama
August 13 Kitaro Tea House
August 29 Kiyose Sunflower Field
September 9 Machida Squirrel Garden
October 15 Kasai-Rinkai Park
November 5 Nitta Shrine
November 26 Isshinyu

INDEX

TOKYO
DAY BY DAY

ENGLISH ADAPTATION: Isabelle Huang
DESIGN & LAYOUT: Adam Grano

Content provided by RETRIP
All information is subject to change

365 days MAINICHI TOKYO
© 2018 RETRIP

First published in Japan in 2018 by Writes Publishing, Inc., Hyogo.

English translation rights arranged with Writes Publishing, Inc. through Tuttle-Mori Agency, Inc., Tokyo.

Printed in South Korea

This edition published by VIZ Media, LLC
P.O. Box 77010
San Francisco, CA 94107

First printing, June 2020

Library of Congress Cataloging-in-Publication Data available.

viz.com